TODAY'S TOP HOME DESIGNS

325

New Home Plans

*Updated Classics
for Today's
Homeowner*

FOR 2006

325 New Home Plans for 2006

hanley▲wood

Published by Hanley Wood
One Thomas Circle, NW, Suite 600
Washington, DC 20005

Distribution Center
29333 Lorie Lane
Wixom, Michigan 48393

Group Vice President, General Manager, Andrew Schultz
Associate Publisher, Editorial Development, Jennifer Pearce
Senior Editor, Nate Ewell
Associate Editor, Simon Hyoun
Senior Plan Merchandiser, Morenci C. Clark
Plan Merchandiser, Nicole Phipps
Proofreader/Copywriter, Dyana Weis
Graphic Artist, Joong Min
Plan Data Team Leader, Susan Jasmin
Production Manager, Brenda McClary

Vice President, Retail Sales, Scott Hill
National Sales Manager, Bruce Holmes
Director, Plan Products, Matt Higgins

Most Hanley Wood titles are available at quantity discounts with bulk purchases for educational, business, or sales promotional use. For information, please contact Bruce Holmes at bholmes@hanleywood.com.

VC Graphics, Inc.
Creative Director, Veronica Vannoy
Graphic Designer, Jennifer Gerstein
Graphic Designer, Denise Reiffenstein

Photo Credits
Upper Right: Design HPK1500014, for details see page 23.
Photo by Mark Englund, courtesy of Lifestyles Home Design Services
Main Photo: Photo by Sam Gray
Back Cover: Photos by Ahmann Design, Inc.

10 9 8 7 6 5 4 3 2 1

Library of Congress Control Number: 2005927710

ISBN #: 1-931131-45-7

325 New Home Plans for 2006

ONLINE EXTRA!

hanley▲wood
Passageway

For access to bonus home plans, articles, online ordering, and more go to: **www.hanleywoodbooks.com/newhomeplans2006**

Features of this site include:

- A dynamic link that lets you search and view bonus home plans
- Online related feature articles
- Built-in tools to save and view your favorite home plans
- A dynamic web link that allows you to order your home plan online
- Contact details for the Hanley Wood Home Plan Hotline
- Free subscriptions to Hanley Wood Home Plan e-news

Something Old,
Some

thing New

Often a gift wrapped in newspaper will contain the best present, whereas the gift encased in shiny paper adorned with frills and bows will be a disappointment. Ideally, a wonderfully decorated package will hold inside the perfect, most thoughtful gift that directly reflects your wishes. That balance between exterior beauty and interior quality is the goal of the new house designs in *325 New Home Plans for 2006*—a goal that is achieved and exceeded.

Building a new home is a gift you give yourself, and is one of the most important purchases you'll ever make. This book is divided into sections based on classic exterior attributes, and is filled with plans enhanced by the latest and greatest trends and amenities. Every plan within is positively outstanding, and each designer has gone to great lengths to make sure your new home is everything you could want and more.

THE WRAPPING

Exterior home design has not changed much over the years. Why fix what isn't broken? Homeowners want their home to have a timeless exterior, one that will fit into existing neighborhoods with ease and maybe even remind them of the house in which they were raised. *325 New Home Plans for 2006* offers an array of exterior designs ranging from vacation-style small homes to expansive, sprawling estates, and everything in between.

An assortment of styles is included in the New Design Showcase, a full-color section of brilliantly designed homes. Flipping through this section may just offer a taste of what's to come—but it would be no surprise if your dream home lies within these pages. Next is a display of Summer Homes and Cottages, followed by Rustic

Getaways and Retreats. Both sections offer cottages, bungalows, and Craftsman-style plans designed to fit perfectly on the water or in the country. For people who thoroughly enjoy their vacation time and are looking for a home that reflects their lifestyles, these pages are a must.

A variety of homes designed for everyone from empty nesters, families large and small, and couples just starting out are arranged into five categories to round out the book. The Farmhouses and Ranches section is filled with plans reflective of this versatile segment of home design. For those looking for a modern spin on home building, take a look through Urban Designs and Traditionals. Homes with Historic Inspiration and English and Provencal Manors will appeal to builders with a penchant for classic design. Sprawling and distinct, the

ABOVE: Flower boxes in the windows and a delicately detailed front porch are special touches to this distinct farmhouse design. See page 15 for floor plans. LEFT: Home theaters are quickly becoming must-have rooms, and are comfortable in any style home.

LEFT: Innovative master bathrooms, like the one shown to the left, can be seen throughout the plans inside—look for luxurious tubs, practical sinks and showers, and tons of storage space!

designs in the Mediterranean and Spanish section are inspirational.

THE GIFT

While homeowners demand timeless, traditional styles for the home's facade, the same can not be said for interior amenities. As the times change, so do new home interiors. The homes in *325 New Home Plans for 2006* include some of the best trends and amenities offered in new home design. The latest room design, space savers and expanders, and the most current technology are all represented.

New homeowners no longer satisfied with just a carved-out space for a washer and dryer are demanding more from their laundry room. Storage space, desks, sinks, and work benches are becoming commonplace in this increasingly

ABOVE: A variety of gables provide great curb appeal to this traditional design—turn to page 24 to see all the surprises inside. OPPOSITE: The door here leads to a private balcony—ideal for homeowners with frequent overnight guests or live-in relatives who deserve their own master suite!

in-demand space. But as they grow in size, so does the importance of discretionary placement—a balance achieved in the new designs within.

Another popular trend in new home plans is the second master suite. This extremely versatile room is ideal for almost any type of homeowner—anyone with visiting parents, children, grandchildren, or friends who love to spend the weekend knows that privacy and a place to feel at home is the greatest gift a host can give her guests. Offering a private bath and some seclusion—some of these rooms are even located near a private balcony or separate entrance—the second master suite is a trend that is here to stay.

As a room or as a space within a room, there is one thing every new home needs in abundance: storage. Look for ample storage space in convenient locations, like walk-in pantries in the kitchen, built-in bookshelves and cabinetry sprinkled discretely throughout the plans, entire attics or bonus rooms that can be solely devoted to storage,

and utility rooms. Eliminating clutter actually may add to the square footage of your living space—and you can't beat that!

The purpose of building new is to get everything exactly right at the start, and this includes planning ahead for the room that is most often remodeled: the bathroom. It may be tempting to skimp on the bathroom to save money, but these plans are designed to include everything you want in a bathroom without sacrificing anything you need. Spa-style tubs, separate bathtubs and showers, dual-sink vanities in a variety of shapes and sizes, plenty of linen storage, and more are trends that will surely endure.

Home automation is an up-and-coming demand sure to appeal to not only the technologically advanced homeowner, but to the buyer interested in protecting his investment. Security systems have come a long way in recent years, and are beginning to gain widespread acceptance. Also attractive is the reality of multi-room audio and lighting options—a luxurious amenity at a surprisingly reasonable price. Wiring your home for these options when you build—whether you're ready to include them or not—will be worth the expense in the long run.

The latest trends are even reaching beyond a home's traditional walls. Outdoor living is an amenity that can be enjoyed in any climate, as long as the proper accoutrements are chosen. Homebuilders in colder climes may want to include an outdoor fireplace instead of the expansive pool and lanai better suited to homes in warmer weather. Entire outdoor kitchens can be enjoyed by all—under a covered porch or under the stars, there's just something special about cooking and dining outdoors.

Sun Soak

Thoughtful details and a superior layout add up to the perfect vacation cottage

A truly original angle offers entrance to this glorious cottage plan, designed to be at home in the country or on the lakefront. One-and-a-half stories and just under 2,100 square feet make a floor plan suited for vacation living. With two bedrooms and two full baths, this is a home that welcomes all who stay here.

Dramatically sloping rooflines are enhanced by two shed dormers, one over the 408-square-foot, front-facing garage. Drop your keys at the table in the foyer and note the winding staircase to the second level, and another to a finished basement. The master bedroom is on the first floor in the center of the plan, with a pampering bath tucked against the garage on the right. A His and Hers walk-in closet provides space for vacation clothes and storage and serves as a buffer between the sleeping area and the bath. A second closet in the bedroom will come in handy, no doubt. Two rear-facing windows bathe the room in natural light.

The master bedroom is separated from the kitchen by a perfectly placed island. A ceiling-height hutch and other space-reclaiming ideas suit the kitchen's mis en place philosophy. Cupboards above and below the lengths of counter space are wonderful attributes of this kitchen, and it's open layout is ideal for passage to the dining room.

RIGHT, Rich wood tones welcome guests into the foyer. LEFT, The fireplace adds to the ambiance of the dining and family rooms—and the spectacular views from the walls of windows are breathtaking.

Photos courtesy of Drummond Designs, Inc.

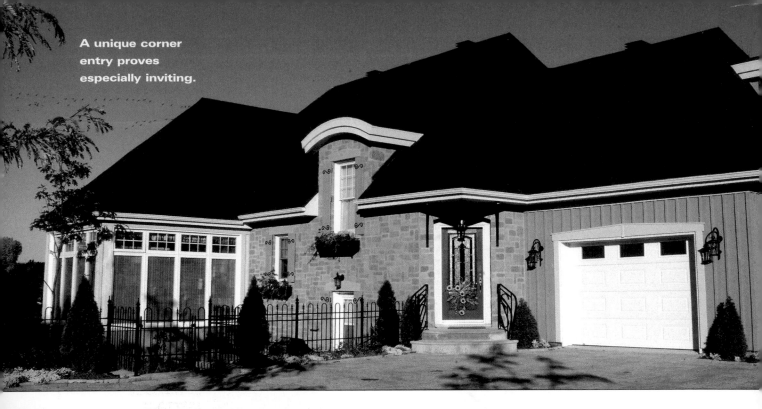

A unique corner entry proves especially inviting.

Light some candles and enjoy a nice long soak in the master bath.

Views from the hallway and kitchen are amazing, as these passageways direct the eyes towards a fireplace dividing the dining room and family room, flanked on either side by window walls. These nearly floor-to-ceiling-height windows pour in natural light during the day, and the moonlight streaming through in the evening will add to the ambiance of these living spaces.

The cozy family room enjoys light not only from the expansive side wall of windows, but from a rear-facing one as well. Kicking back and relaxing is the order of the day in this space, ideal for entertaining family and guests in comfort while enjoying the glow of the fireplace when the sun goes down.

Encased in full-length glass windows and with a door leading to the outdoor surroundings, a sundeck is a wonderful addition to this vacation design. Accessed from the dining room, this is a great place to start your day with that morning cup of coffee, or cap of a meal with an after dinner drink.

The second floor has another bedroom and full bath, perfect for weekend guests at this retreat. The luxury of not only a private room with a bumped-out window enjoying the same side-facing views as the family room, but of an entire level almost solely devoted to this suite will surely be appreciated by visitors. A study rounds out this level and can be used by owners to pay bills or file paperwork.

The basement can be finished at any time to include another bedroom with walk-in closet, a half-bath, another family room, and—best of all—a game room. Ample storage space off the gaming area is another bonus.

Plan;

HPK1500001

Style:
EUROPEAN COTTAGE

First Floor:
1,488 SQ. FT.

Second Floor:
602 SQ. FT.

Total:
2,090 SQ. FT.

Basement:
1,321 SQ. FT.

Bedrooms:
2

Bathrooms:
2

Width:
60' - 0"

Depth:
44' - 0"

Foundation:
FINISHED BASEMENT

Second Floor

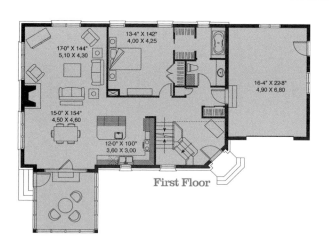

First Floor

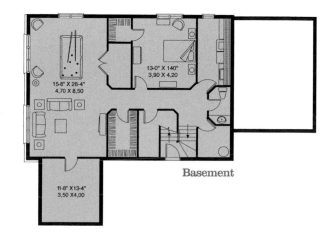

Basement

For more detailed information, please check the floor plans carefully.

Plan:
HPK1500007

Style:
COUNTRY COTTAGE

First Floor:
2,589 SQ. FT.

Second Floor:
981 SQ. FT.

Total:
3,570 SQ. FT.

Bedrooms:
4

Bathrooms:
3 1/2

Width:
70' - 8"

Depth:
61' - 10"

Foundation:
CRAWLSPACE

The horizontal siding of this facade evokes a sense of charm and comfort similar to a log cabin. The covered porch opens to a foyer, flanked by a study on the left and the dining room on the right. Beyond the foyer sits the living room, complete with a fireplace and double-door access to the large rear deck. To the right of the living room, a second fireplace in the family room warms the large country kitchen, and the nearby utility room and office. An island snack bar in the kitchen conveniently serves the family room. On the opposite side of the floor plan, the master suite offers a private entrance to the rear deck, His and Hers walk-in closets, a dual sink vanity, a compartmented toilet, a separate shower, and a garden tub. Upstairs, three family bedrooms, each with a walk-in closet, share two full baths.

First Floor

Second Floor

New Design Showcase

Plan:
HPK1500008

Style:
CONTEMPORARY

First Floor:
1,279 SQ. FT.

Second Floor:
1,114 SQ. FT.

Total:
2,393 SQ. FT.

Bonus Space:
337 SQ. FT.

Bedrooms:
4

Bathrooms:
2

Width:
68' - 0"

Depth:
36' - 0"

Foundation:
SLAB

Rear Exterior

Covered porches in the front and rear of this contemporary design serve to facilitate a smooth indoor/outdoor relationship. First-floor living spaces are wide open—you'll never miss a word of conversation if you're cooking in the kitchen and serving friends and family in hearth-warmed family room or informal dining area nearby. Also on this level are the laundry room and a full bath. Venture upstairs to find four family bedrooms, each with a spacious closet, and another full bath. Dual sinks in this bathroom help ease the chaos of morning/bedtime rituals.

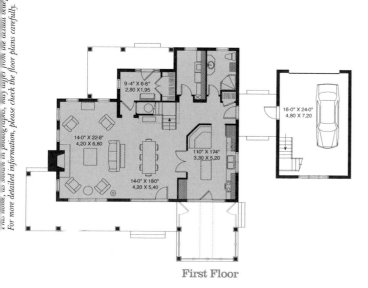

First Floor

Second Floor

Plan:
HPK1500009

Style:
COUNTRY COTTAGE

Square Footage:
1,644

Bonus Space:
922 SQ. FT.

Bedrooms:
3

Bathrooms:
2

Width:
63' - 0"

Depth:
52' - 2"

Foundation:
CRAWLSPACE, SLAB, UNFINISHED BASEMENT

Looking for a flexible home? This is it: a comfortable one-level Cape Cod with future space built into the design. The entire second floor is dedicated to fitting your family as needed. The complete first floor boasts two family bedrooms sharing a full bath, an open kitchen with an adjoining dining bay, and a capacious great room with rear-porch access and a warm fireplace. The master suite enjoys privacy and a full bath.

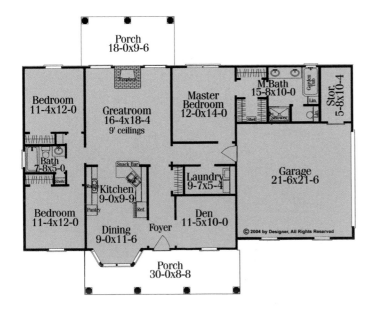

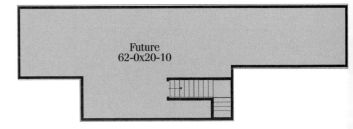

New Design Showcase

Plan:
HPK1500010

Style:
CONTEMPORARY

First Floor:
1,274 SQ. FT.

Second Floor:
1,009 SQ. FT.

Total:
2,283 SQ. FT.

Bedrooms:
3

Bathrooms:
2 1/2

Width:
50' - 0"

Depth:
46' - 0"

Foundation:
UNFINISHED BASEMENT

Special attention to exterior details and interior nuances gives this relaxed farmhouse fine distinction on any street. From the large covered porch, enter to find a spacious, thoughtful plan. A striking central staircase separates the first-floor living area, which boasts a home office and a cathedral ceiling in the living room. The second floor includes a master suite, two secondary bedrooms that share a full bath, and a flexible upstairs sitting area. The master suite contains a bath with a double-bowl vanity and a walk-in closet.

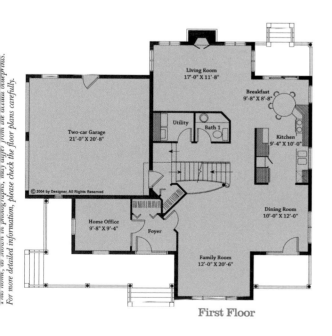

First Floor

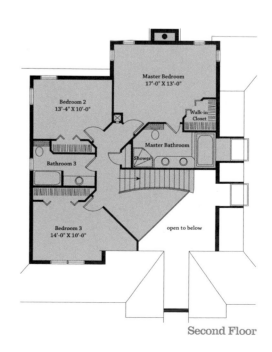

Second Floor

Plan:
HPK1500305

Style:
TRADITIONAL

First Floor:
1,178 SQ. FT.

Second Floor:
1,321 SQ. FT.

Total:
2,499 SQ. FT.

Bedrooms:
4

Bathrooms:
2

Width:
50' - 0"

Depth:
44' - 0"

Foundation:
SLAB

A stone masonry facade and arched windows grace the exterior of this house, with Palladian glass dappling the sunlight on the inside. A flexible room on the main floor provides a possibility of five bedrooms in all. Laundry and bath are located behind the flex room, with kitchen, formal dining room, and family room forming one large area. A pantry and drop zone are secreted in the center of this level. Upstairs reside the remaining bedrooms (look at all of the walk-in closet space!), two more baths, linen closet, and perspective to the entry way below. The inhabitant of the master suite will live like royalty amidst its spaciousness.

First Floor

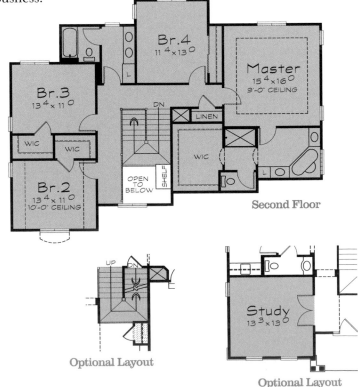

Second Floor

Optional Layout

Optional Layout

Plan:
HPK1500306

Style:
CRAFTSMAN

First Floor:
3,649 SQ. FT.

Second Floor:
1,302 SQ. FT.

Total:
4,951 SQ. FT.

Bedrooms:
4

Bathrooms:
3 1/2 + 1/2

Width:
88' - 4"

Depth:
82' - 9"

Foundation:
FINISHED BASEMENT, UNFINISHED BASEMENT

The air of an English Country manor is re-created throughtout this home. Repeating interior arches, stone walls, and beamed ceilings are reminiscent of a home created a half century ago. Highlights include an inviting outdoor summer living room with stone floor, fireplace, wood-beamed ceiling, and the magnificent view it offers. Other exciting features include a large gathering space with kitchen/breakfast room, butler/wine gallery, pub, and hearth room. Views from the entry include the great room, formal dining room, and a library with double doors and built-ins. The first-floor master bedroom pampers with luxury; three upper-level bedrooms—each with private access to a bath and large walk-in closets—make this home the perfect fit for your family.

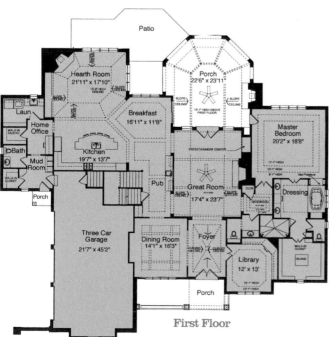

First Floor

Second Floor

325 New Home Plans

New Design Showcase

Plan:
HPK1500301

Style:
EUROPEAN COTTAGE

Main Level:
2,551 SQ. FT.

Lower Level:
2,028 SQ. FT.

Total:
4,579 SQ. FT.

Bedrooms:
4

Bathrooms:
3

Width:
89' - 4"

Depth:
67' - 0"

Foundation:
FINISHED BASEMENT

Reap the best of three building styles in one resplendent home. A three-car garage preserves the majesty of the exterior, adjoining one of a grand total of three porches. Your home's front hallway is topped with an inviting plant ledge, cathedral ceiling, and a profusion of natural light. Both master and upper-level baths contain glassed-in showers and separate tubs. The openness and functionality of the kitchen area is highlighted by the walk-in pantry, snack bar, and prep island, and leads to your formal dining room. The great room and master suite perpetuate the feeling of self-contained luxury. The top floor is reserved for bedrooms three and four, more entertaining (impress with recreation AND media rooms!), and storage. Leave the bustle inside as you escape to your private patio/deck through the master suite, or gaze through a series of arched windows with expansive rear and front views.

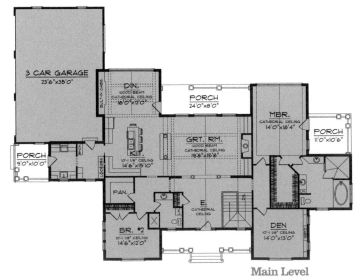

Main Level

Lower Level

Plan:
HPK1500012

Style:
TRADITIONAL

Main Level:
2,055 SQ. FT.

Lower Level:
1,854 SQ. FT.

Total:
3,909 SQ. FT.

Bedrooms:
4

Bathrooms:
2 1/2 + 1/2

Width:
77' - 4"

Depth:
62' - 4"

Foundation:
FINISHED WALKOUT BASEMENT

Rustic blends with traditional styling, creating a distinctive facade. Inside, a contemporary layout aims to provide room-to-room flow. A decorative ceiling highlights the great room that connects to the open dining room. A large snack island facing the dining room and adjoining hearth room accommodates casual eating, while a huge walk-in pantry makes this space more efficient. A first-floor master suite shares comfortable amentities in the roomy bath and oversized walk-in closet. A lower level houses the secondary bedrooms, large recreation room, wet bar, built-ins, and walk-out porch for guests and family members to enjoy.

Main Level

Lower Level

Plan:
HPK1500303

Style:
EUROPEAN COTTAGE

Main Level:
3,394 SQ. FT.

Lower Level:
2,966 SQ. FT.

Total:
6,360 SQ. FT.

Bedrooms:
4

Bathrooms:
3 1/2 + 1/2

Width:
94' - 0"

Depth:
82' - 0"

Foundation:
FINISHED WALKOUT BASEMENT

A turret with conical roof and spire sets the tone for this country manor. Hide a grand total of three vehicles at the front of the house, then ascend to your throne discretely, or make a more public entrance through the grand foyer to your castle. Built-in art niches and cabinets, as well as columns and a fireplace, greet you inside. Feast like a king or queen in your kitchen with walk-in pantry, snack bar, and island, or gather your court in the formal dining room. Afterwards, repair to the craft, theater, or rec rooms upstairs. Three bedrooms are tucked safely behind the family room, housing all of your treasure in privacy, splendor, and comfort.

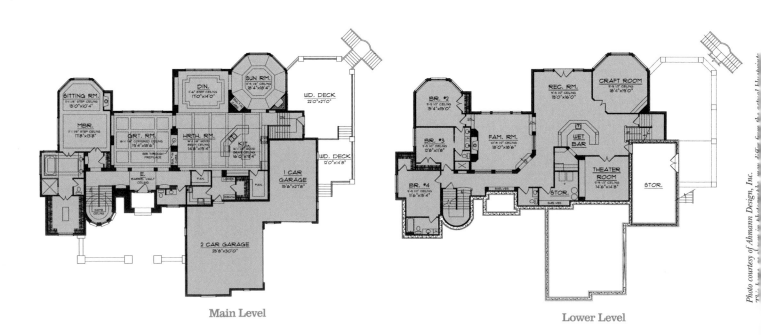

Main Level

Lower Level

Photo courtesy of Ahmann Design, Inc.

Plan:
HPK1500004

Style:
FRENCH

Square Footage:
1,902

Bedrooms:
3

Bathrooms:
2 ¹/₂

Width:
84' - 7"

Depth:
34' - 5"

Foundation:
SLAB

Decidely country, this estate is designed to take advantage of pastoral views front and rear. Fine columns grace the covered front porch that creates an enjoyable extended living space. A tiled entry gives way to a open gallery that expertly guides you through the floor plan. To the left, the master wing houses the private master suite featuring a secluded patio, amentity-filled bath, and a spacious walk-in closet with built-ins. To the right, secondary bedrooms—one with a bay window—share a full bath. At the rear of the home, the oversized great room is a hub of warmth with its extended-hearth fireplace. Within steps, the country kitchen unfolds into an attractive workhorse meant for entertaining and cooking.

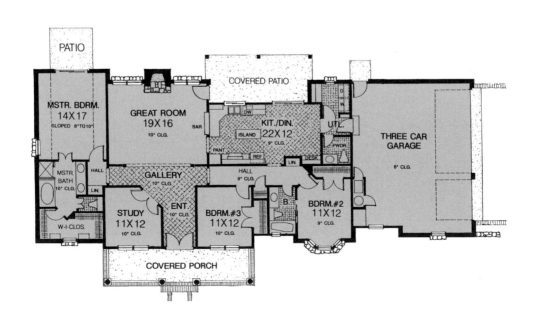

Plan:
HPK1500013

Style:
GEORGIAN

First Floor:
1,773 SQ. FT.

Second Floor:
709 SQ. FT.

Total:
2,482 SQ. FT.

Bedrooms:
4

Bathrooms:
2 1/2

Width:
54' - 0"

Depth:
47' - 6"

Foundation:
**SLAB,
UNFINISHED
WALKOUT
BASEMENT**

This two-story traditional home offers space for everyone. A handsome brick exterior, keystone arches, and an attractive shed dormer provide tons of curb appeal. The foyer is flanked by a study and the dining room. To the rear are the more casual spaces. The grand room features two-story ceilings, a fireplace, and is within steps of the island kitchen and breakfast room. The first-floor master suite is convenient as well as secluded, and offers walk-in closets, a full bath, and tray ceiling. Upstairs, three roomy secondary bedrooms—two with walk-in closets—share a full bath.

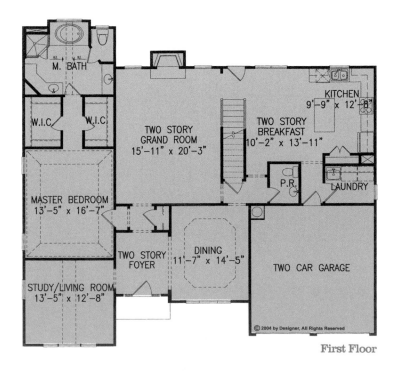

First Floor

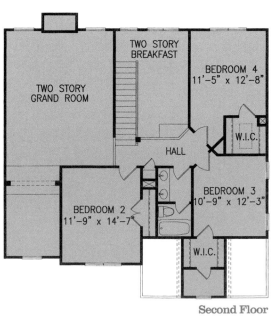

Second Floor

Plan:
HPK1500014

Style:
COLONIAL

First Floor:
1,368 SQ. FT.

Second Floor:
1,140 SQ. FT.

Total:
2,508 SQ. FT.

Bedrooms:
4

Bathrooms:
2 ¹/₂

Width:
62' - 0"

Depth:
48' - 0"

Foundation:
UNFINISHED BASEMENT

Three dormers on a side-gable roof and classic fenestration establish a pleasing Colonial style to this home's facade. The attention to the entryway and second-floor balcony are finer touches owners will appreciate. The interior offers an uncomplicated layout—gathering spaces on the lower floor and sleeping quarters above. The family room enjoys a majestic fireplace and incredible views through the intimate bay window.

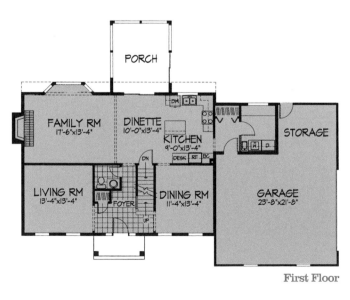

First Floor

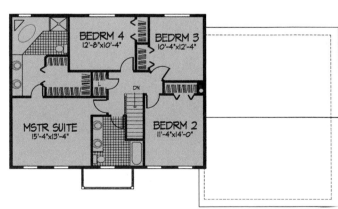

Second Floor

This home, as shown in photographs, may differ from the actual blueprints. For more detailed information, please check the floor plans carefully.

325
New Home Plans

New Design Showcase

Plan:
HPK1500015

Style:
TIDEWATER

First Floor:
1,595 SQ. FT.

Second Floor:
1,600 SQ. FT.

Total:
3,195 SQ. FT.

Bedrooms:
5

Bathrooms:
4

Width:
54' - 0"

Depth:
43' - 0"

Foundation:
UNFINISHED WALKOUT BASEMENT, SLAB

Cedar shingles are brightened by a stone-covered entrance, decorative porch anchors, and five open gables—a winning combination from the curb. The interior layout is functional for entertaining and for family-focused living. A formal dining room features a lovely archway, which the living room echoes from across the gorgeous two-story foyer. A private guest room, or study, is conveniently positioned near a full bath. The C-shaped kitchen offers an island and an open breakfast area. The grand room, only steps away, provides a great view of the fireplace. The second floor is complete with three family bedrooms and two full baths. An elegant gallery overlook sits between the bedrooms and the master suite. Variety spices up the master bedroom with a sitting area, optional fireplace, and an amenity-filled bath, oversized walk-in closet, and optional exercise or craft room addition.

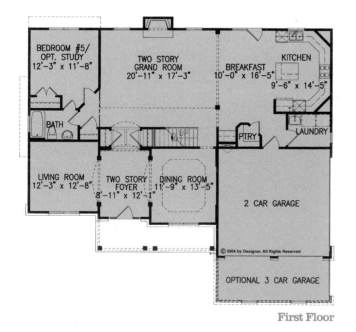

First Floor

Second Floor

Photo courtesy of Garrell Associates, Inc.
This home, as shown in photographs, may differ from the actual blueprints.

Plan:
HPK1500016

Style:
FARMHOUSE

First Floor:
1,156 SQ. FT.

Second Floor:
988 SQ. FT.

Total:
2,144 SQ. FT.

Bedrooms:
4

Bathrooms:
2 1/2

Width:
70' - 0"

Depth:
60' - 0"

Foundation:
UNFINISHED BASEMENT

A wraparound porch and symmetrical facade effect a warm curbside presence for this country-style two-story. Inside, an uncomplicated layout establishes shared spaces on the first floor—including a family room with fireplace—and sleeping quarters on the second floor. The master suite is accompanied by a generous walk-in closet and full bath. The remaining three bedrooms share a full bath among them.

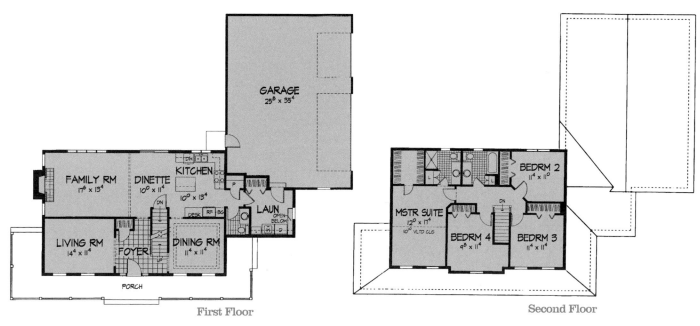

This home, as shown in photographs, may differ from the actual blueprints. For more detailed information, please check the floor plans carefully.

First Floor

Second Floor

Plan:
HPK1500307

Style:
MEDITERRANEAN

First Floor:
2,074 SQ. FT.

Second Floor:
1,214 SQ. FT.

Total:
3,288 SQ. FT.

Bedrooms:
4

Bathrooms:
3 ¹/₂

Width:
77' - 8"

Depth:
60' - 0"

Foundation:
UNFINISHED BASEMENT

This nostalgic villa with front portico also has an attached three-car garage for modern-day convenience. The front entry is graced with a two-story ceiling for exceptional grandeur. An arched entry leads to a spectacular convergence of the kitchen, breakfast nook, and great room (below another two-story ceiling). The breakfast nook looks onto a two-sided deck. The master suite is also located downstairs, along with utility area and sitting room. Upstairs are found three additional bedrooms and two lofts. Those two-story ceilings provide great vantage points to the entry way and great room below. Mediterranean luxury throughout!

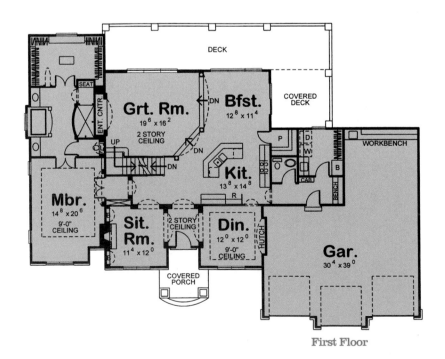

First Floor

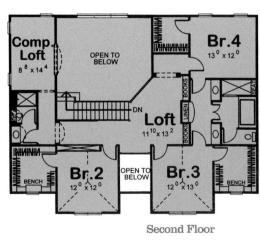

Second Floor

Plan:
HPK1500017

Style:
CONTEMPORARY

First Floor:
2,292 SQ. FT.

Second Floor:
925 SQ. FT.

Total:
3,217 SQ. FT.

Bedrooms:
3

Bathrooms:
3 ¹/2

Width:
70' - 0"

Depth:
71' - 0"

Foundation:
**CRAWLSPACE,
FINISHED
BASEMENT,
SLAB**

Rear Exterior

Front Exterior

An abundance of windows provides a wealth of natural light throughout this Contemporary home. A covered patio offers French-door access to the two-story dining room. The great room sits at the heart of the home with a corner fireplace and built-in media center. The home office is appropriately placed adjacent to the lavish master suite. The rear patio boasts a built-in BBQ pit ideal for outdoor entertaining. Upstairs houses two additional family bedrooms with full baths and a library with built-in amenities.

First Floor

Second Floor

Plan:
HPK1500018

Style:
ITALIANATE

First Floor:
2,782 SQ. FT.

Second Floor:
401 SQ. FT.

Total:
3,183 SQ. FT.

Bedrooms:
3

Bathrooms:
4

Width:
65' - 0"

Depth:
84' - 2"

Foundation:
SLAB

Spanish and Mediterranean influences emanate from both the facade and the outdoor living spaces in this home. An arch motif echoes throughout the house on windows and doorways. Decorative ceilings grace the master bedroom, living room, and dining room. A breathtaking covered patio featuring an outdoor kitchen area is accessed by rooms throughout the house, and will be the perfect spot from which to entertain and enjoy views. A second-story loft includes a full bath and closet.

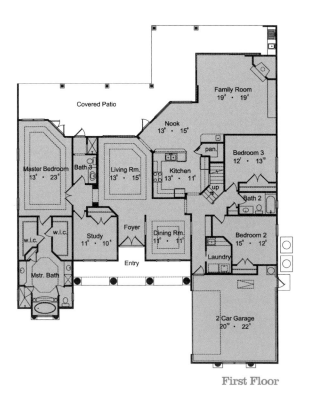

First Floor

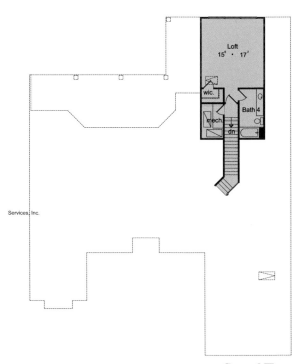

Second Floor

Plan:
HPK1500302

Style:
EUROPEAN COTTAGE

Main Level:
2,262 SQ. FT.

Lower Level:
2,195 SQ. FT.

Total:
4,457 SQ. FT.

Bedrooms:
4

Bathrooms:
3 ¹/₂

Width:
76' - 0"

Depth:
59' - 4"

Foundation:
FINISHED BASEMENT

Live like a king in your European Country manor. Attention-grabbing columns grace the main entrance as well as the twin double-garages. Wait until your guests step inside and see the arches, step ceilings, wood paneling, and more columns, as well as built-in cabinets for the den. Stone masonry tastefully houses your wine collection and displays the wet bar, while paneling ensconces your fireplace and great/family room in luxury. Three bedrooms and two baths, as well as a storage room, are tucked away upstairs, leaving room to entertain, exercise, or enjoy a private viewing in your home theater. A covered deck at the rear allows you to survey your domain.

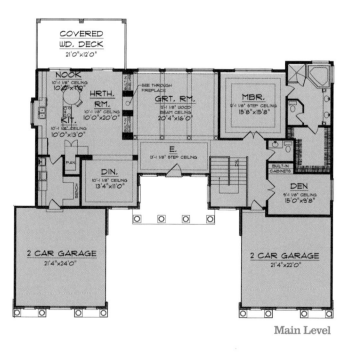

Main Level

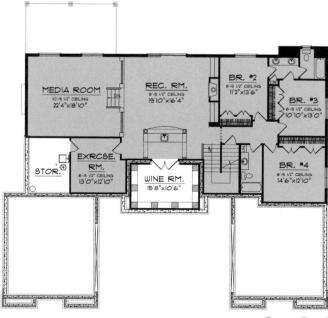

Lower Level

Plan:
HPK1500019

Style:
ITALIANATE

First Floor:
3,240 SQ. FT.

Second Floor:
1,215 SQ. FT.

Total:
4,455 SQ. FT.

Bedrooms:
4

Bathrooms:
3 ¹/₂

Width:
65' - 0"

Depth:
99' - 0"

Foundation:
SLAB

A pleasing old-world Spanish design conjures stylish California and Florida neighborhoods of the 1930s. Magnificent ceiling details can be found in the foyer, study, master suite, and dining room. A modern open kitchen features a large island and a smaller central island that creates plenty of space and work room for the family. The family and eating nook each are open to the kitchen and offer views of the covered patio, which features a mini-kitchen and pool bath. Three family bedrooms—two upstairs—a loft, and a media room provide room for guests and family privacy.

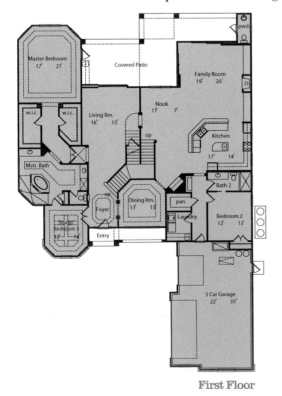

First Floor

Second Floor

Plan:
HPK1500002

Style:
EUROPEAN COTTAGE

First Floor:
837 SQ. FT.

Second Floor:
890 SQ. FT.

Total:
1,727 SQ. FT.

Bedrooms:
3

Bathrooms:
2

Width:
36' - 0"

Depth:
39' - 8"

Foundation:
UNFINISHED BASEMENT

With stucco accents, hipped rooflines, and graceful details, this fine two-story home will be a delight to live in. The foyer acts as an air lock, preventing cold breezes from reaching the living areas. A two-story living room is to the right of the foyer and offers a warming fireplace. At the rear of the home, the efficient open kitchen offers a worktop island with snack bar, and a window sink. Upstairs, three bedrooms—each with walk-in closets—share a spacious bath. One bedroom provides a small, private sitting room.

First Floor

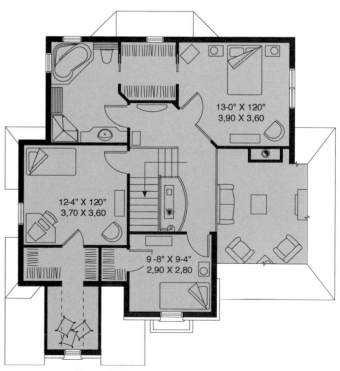

Second Floor

Plan:
HPK1500020

Style:
CONTEMPORARY

Main Level:
3,663 SQ. FT.

Upper Level:
881 SQ. FT.

Lower Level:
4,483 SQ. FT.

Total:
9,027 SQ. FT.

Bonus Space:
821 SQ. FT.

Bedrooms:
7

Bathrooms:
6 1/2 + 1/2

Width:
86' - 4"

Depth:
98' - 4"

Foundation:
FINISHED WALKOUT BASEMENT

The three-level design finds inspiration in the resort spas of the 19th Century and places a luxurious, well-lit indoor pool on the lower level. A nearby exercise room also encourages healthy living, and the theater at the rear of the plan delivers relaxation. A total of seven bedrooms occupy the outer parts of the plan, while a large living room, dining room, and kitchen dominate its center. The upper level suite enjoys complete privacy and great views from the exclusive balcony.

Main Level

Upper Level

Lower Level

© The Sater Design Collection, Inc.

Plan:
HPK1500021

Style:
COUNTRY COTTAGE

First Floor:
2,159 SQ. FT.

Second Floor:
1,160 SQ. FT.

Total:
3,319 SQ. FT.

Bonus Space:
317 SQ. FT.

Bedrooms:
5

Bathrooms:
5

Width:
63' - 0"

Depth:
114' - 10"

Foundation:
PIER (SAME AS PILING)

Triple dormers and a widow's walk set off the standing-seam roof of this New South cottage, inspired by island plantation houses of the early 20th Century. Horizontal siding lends an informal character to the stately facade, which is set off by massive columns and tall shuttered windows. A midlevel landing eases the transition to an L-shaped plan anchored by a forward arrangement of the great room and study. The foyer creates a fluid boundary by connecting the entry veranda with the wrapping rear veranda, pool, and spa. Toward the center of the plan, a winding staircase defines a progresssion from the public realm, which includes a high-tech kitchen and a formal dining room, and the private sleeping quarters. Luxury amenities highlight the master retreat, which offers its own acccss to the solana and pool.

First Floor

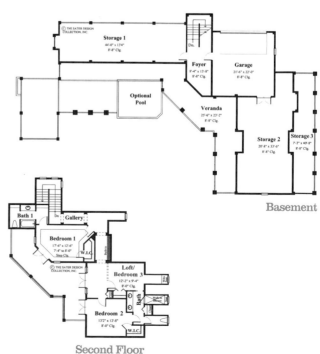

Basement

Second Floor

Plan:
HPK1500003

Style:
CRAFTSMAN

Square Footage:
1,847

Bedrooms:
3

Bathrooms:
2

Width:
34' - 0"

Depth:
76' - 0"

Foundation:
CRAWLSPACE, UNFINISHED WALKOUT BASEMENT

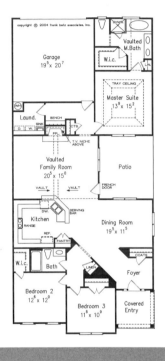

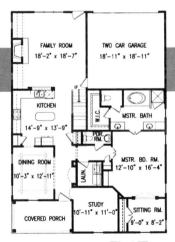

First Floor

Plan:
HPK1500005

Style:	Total:	Width:
CRAFTSMAN	**2,272 SQ. FT.**	**38' - 0"**
First Floor:	Bedrooms:	Depth:
1,587 SQ. FT.	**3**	**55' - 0"**
Second Floor:	Bathrooms:	Foundation:
685 SQ. FT.	**2 ½**	**SLAB**

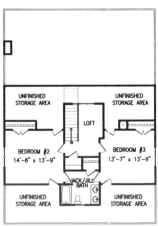

Second Floor

Plan:
HPK1500330

Style:
CRAFTSMAN

First Floor:
1,294 SQ. FT.

Second Floor:
1,220 SQ. FT.

Total:
2,514 SQ. FT.

Bonus Space:
366 SQ. FT.

Bedrooms:
4

Bathrooms:
3 ¹/2

Width:
38' - 0"

Depth:
76' - 0"

Foundation:
UNFINISHED BASEMENT

The unassuming facade of this traditional home offers few clues about how ideal this deisgn is for entertaining. The lack of unnecessary walls achieves a clean, smart layout that flows seamlessly. A side deck accessed from the living room and breakfast area extends the gathering outside. Upstairs houses all of the family bedrooms, including the master suite, enhanced by a spacious private deck. Two additional family bedrooms share a full bath. A fourth bedroom boasts a full bath and could be used as a recreation/exercise/guest room. The central study/loft area is perfect for a family computer.

First Floor

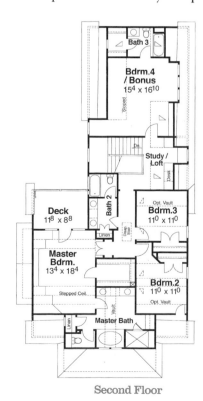

Second Floor

Optional Layout

Summer Homes
& Cottages

Plan:
HPK1500024

Style:
COUNTRY COTTAGE

First Floor:
1,766 SQ. FT.

Second Floor:
1,582 SQ. FT.

Total:
3,348 SQ. FT.

Bonus Space:
434 SQ. FT.

Bedrooms:
4

Bathrooms:
4 1/2

Width:
56' - 0"

Depth:
80' - 0"

Foundation:
PIER (SAME AS PILING)

© The Sater Design Collection, Inc.

Wide verandas and a double portico enrich the sidewalk presentation of this coastal cottage. Influenced by the raffish dialects of breezy Key West styles, this Revival home integrates regional elements with world-class components, such as a cathedral ceiling in the gathering room and a gallery loft that links to the forward portico. The entry hall leads through a centered gallery, defined by columns and graceful arches, which eases the transition from the outdoors to a space-age media room, equipped with an up-to-the minute entertainment center and built-in cabinetry. A flex room connects the service entry and utility zone with an angled hall and luxe bedroom suite. On the upper level, French doors open the gathering room to a wide veranda.

First Floor

Second Floor

Summer Homes & Cottages

325

New Home Plans

© The Sater Design Collection, Inc.

Plan:
HPK1500025

Style:
COUNTRY COTTAGE
First Floor:
1,372 SQ. FT.
Second Floor:
1,617 SQ. FT.
Total:
2,989 SQ. FT.
Bedrooms:
5
Bathrooms:
5 1/2
Width:
50' - 0"
Depth:
83' - 10"
Foundation:
PIER (SAME AS PILING)

Sun-kissed porticos and wide-open decks capture views and permit breezes to whisper through rooms all around this coastal cottage. Inspired by Caribbean manors and refined in the architecture of Charleston Row houses, the style is brought into the 21st Century with a highly functional floor plan that is fully engaged with the outdoors. The foyer links the entry with public living spaces as well as a private room that flexes to accommodate guests or harbor a quiet library or conservatory. Built-in cabinetry and a stepped ceiling subdue the scale of the media room. The central stairs create a fluid connection with the spacious living room, formal dining room, and kitchen. An upper veranda features an alfresco kitchen that extends the function of the dining room.

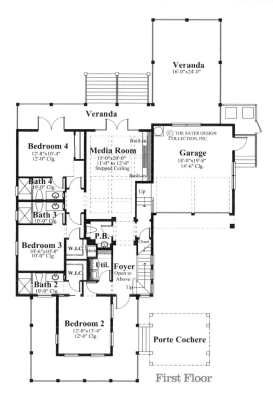

First Floor

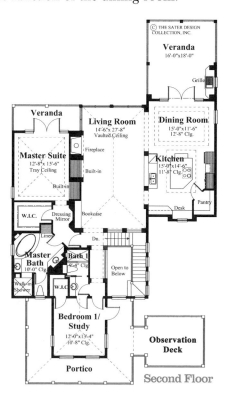

Second Floor

ORDER BLUEPRINTS 24 HOURS, 7 DAYS A WEEK, AT 1-800-521-6797 OR EPLANS.COM

37

Plan:
HPK1500026

Style:
CONTEMPORARY

First Floor:
908 SQ. FT.

Second Floor:
576 SQ. FT.

Total:
1,484 SQ. FT.

Bedrooms:
3

Bathrooms:
2

Width:
26' - 0"

Depth:
48' - 0"

Foundation:
UNFINISHED BASEMENT

First Floor

Second Floor

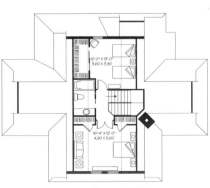

First Floor

Plan:
HPK1500027

Style:	Total:	Width:
VACATION	**1,832 SQ. FT.**	**38' - 0"**
First Floor:	Bedrooms:	Depth:
1,212 SQ. FT.	**3**	**40' - 0"**
Second Floor:	Bathrooms:	Foundation:
620 SQ. FT.	**2**	**UNFINISHED BASEMENT**

Second Floor

Plan:
HPK1500028

Style:
CONTEMPORARY

First Floor:
1,301 SQ. FT.

Second Floor:
652 SQ. FT.

Total:
1,953 SQ. FT.

Bonus Space:
372 SQ. FT.

Bedrooms:
3

Bathrooms:
2 1/2

Width:
58' - 0"

Depth:
55' - 0"

Foundation:
UNFINISHED BASEMENT

Seeing this home is believing in the perfection of vacation-house design. Three sets of French doors provide entrance to three different rooms at the front of the home. Gorgeous sets of stairs surrounding a turreted two-story atrium also lead to a second-level balcony—one of two—so homeowners can truly enjoy the views and atmosphere of their surroundings. Abundant windows allow natural light inside. The master suite and bath are a study in lavishness, and are located on the first floor. Two more bedrooms share a full bath on the second level. Also upstairs are a generous amount of bonus space to finish as you see fit, a two-story office, and a sitting room.

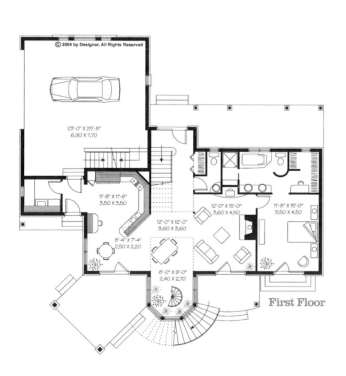

First Floor

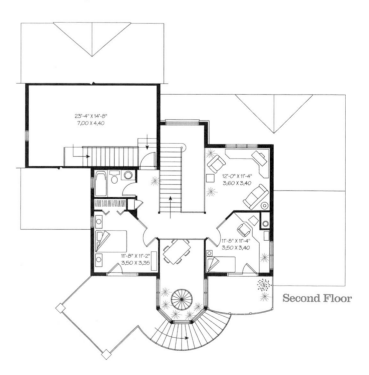

Second Floor

325 Summer Homes & Cottages
New Home Plans

Plan:
HPK1500029

Style:
FLORIDIAN

First Floor:
1,000 SQ. FT.

Second Floor:
958 SQ. FT.

Third Floor:
178 SQ. FT.

Total:
2,136 SQ. FT.

Bedrooms:
2

Bathrooms:
3 ½

Width:
31' - 4"

Depth:
52' - 0"

Foundation:
CRAWLSPACE

Beach living at its finest—this plan offers all of the amenities of a primary residence. Inside, front and rear porches on two levels mean you are never far from the view. The master bedroom, with private access to a rear porch, is warmed by a central fireplace. A convenient morning kitchen at the entrance of the master bedroom makes breakfast in bed an option everyday. A second bedroom on this level is complete with a full bath. The outdoor shower is an added bonus. The second level, warmed by a second fireplace, features an open floor plan perfect for entertaining. Flex space with a large walk-in closet is connected to a full bath and could be used as a guest suite. The third level will surely be a family favorite. A cupola beach view, sleeping loft, morning kitchen, and private balcony make this area a relaxing retreat.

First Floor

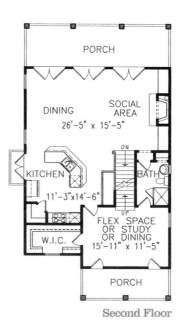

Second Floor

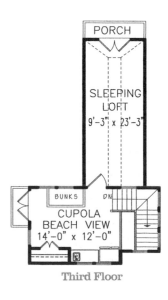

Third Floor

Plan:
HPK1500030

Style:
CONTEMPORARY

First Floor:
1,024 SQ. FT.

Second Floor:
456 SQ. FT.

Total:
1,480 SQ. FT.

Bedrooms:
2

Bathrooms:
2

Width:
32' - 0"

Depth:
40' - 0"

Foundation:
UNFINISHED BASEMENT

A conservative and charming traditional plan delivers easy living and awaits a personal touch. The two-story great room and dining area handles family gatherings, apart from the master bedroom at the top of the plan. The second bedroom resides upstairs, along with a reading room or media room. Full baths accompany both bedrooms. A classic front porch frames the entryway and brings interest to the cross-gabled design. A small mudroom/utility space receives traffic from the rear entry.

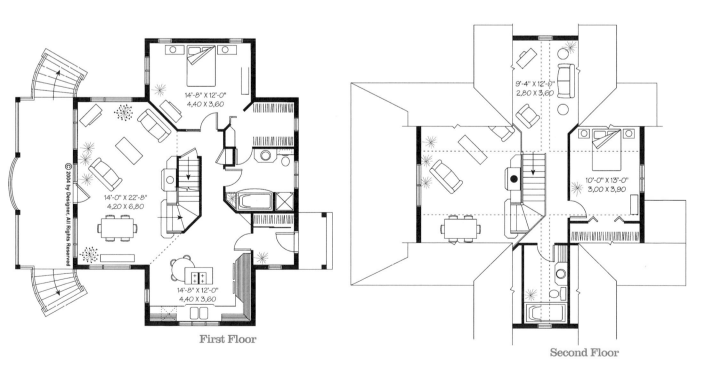

First Floor

Second Floor

© 2004 by Designer, All Rights Reserved

Plan:
HPK1500031

Style:
CONTEMPORARY

First Floor:
728 SQ. FT.

Second Floor:
420 SQ. FT.

Total:
1,148 SQ. FT.

Bedrooms:
1

Bathrooms:
1 1/2

Width:
28' - 0"

Depth:
26' - 0"

Foundation:
UNFINISHED BASEMENT

First Floor

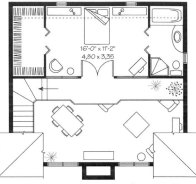

Second Floor

Plan:
HPK1500032

Style:
CRAFTSMAN

Square Footage:
1,393

Bonus Space:
160 SQ. FT.

Bedrooms:
2

Bathrooms:
2

Width:
32' - 0"

Depth:
63' - 0"

Foundation:
UNFINISHED WALKOUT BASEMENT, SLAB

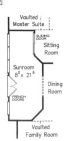

Optional Layout

ORDER BLUEPRINTS 24 HOURS, 7 DAYS A WEEK, AT 1-800-521-6797 OR EPLANS.COM

Plan:
HPK1500033

Style:
COUNTRY COTTAGE

Square Footage:
1,546

Bedrooms:
2

Bathrooms:
2

Width:
37' - 0"

Depth:
64' - 0"

Foundation:
SLAB

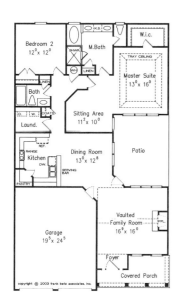

Plan:
HPK1500034

Style:
COUNTRY COTTAGE

Square Footage:
1,627

Bedrooms:
3

Bathrooms:
2

Width:
37' - 0"

Depth:
66' - 0"

Foundation:
SLAB

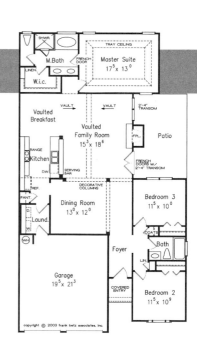

Plan:
HPK1500035

Style:
CAPE COD

First Floor:
772 SQ. FT.

Second Floor:
523 SQ. FT.

Total:
1,295 SQ. FT.

Bedrooms:
2

Bathrooms:
2

Width:
26' - 0"

Depth:
30' - 0"

Foundation:
UNFINISHED BASEMENT

First Floor

Second Floor

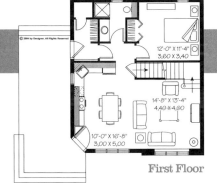

First Floor

Plan:
HPK1500036

Style:	Total:	Width:
CONTEMPORARY	**1,295 SQ. FT.**	**26' - 0"**
First Floor:	Bedrooms:	Depth:
772 SQ. FT.	**2**	**30' - 0"**
Second Floor:	Bathrooms:	Foundation:
523 SQ. FT.	**2**	**UNFINISHED BASEMENT**

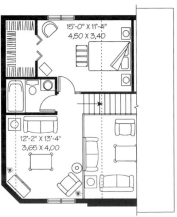

Second Floor

Plan:
HPK1500308

Style:
COUNTRY COTTAGE

First Floor:
2,037 SQ. FT.

Second Floor:
596 SQ. FT.

Total:
2,633 SQ. FT.

Bedrooms:
3

Bathrooms:
3

Width:
42' - 0"

Depth:
75' - 0"

Foundation:
SLAB, UNFINISHED BASEMENT

This beautiful home offers angles and varied ceiling heights throughout. The great room showcases these elements and enjoys access to the covered porch and a view to the rear yard. Interior and exterior fireplaces provide a cozy atmoshpere. Enjoyment of the great room expands into the formal dining area. The master bedroom suite offers an 11-foot ceiling, a luxurious bath, and access to the covered porch are delightful surprises. Split stairs overlook the gallery and lead to the second-floor loft, full bath, and bonus room.

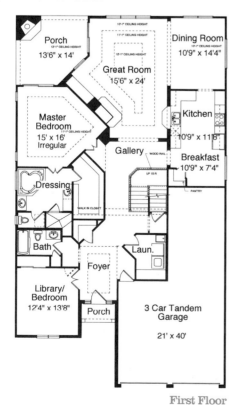

First Floor

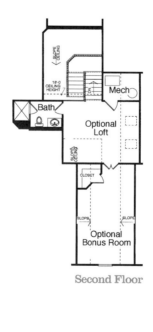

Second Floor

Plan:
HPK1500037

Style:
CRAFTSMAN

Square Footage:
1,407

Bedrooms:
2

Bathrooms:
2

Width:
32' - 0"

Depth:
61' - 7"

Foundation:
**SLAB,
UNFINISHED
WALKOUT
BASEMENT**

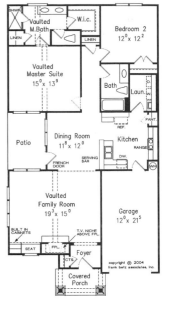

Optional Layout

Plan:
HPK1500038

Style:
**COUNTRY
COTTAGE**

Square Footage:
996

Bedrooms:
3

Bathrooms:
1

Width:
24' - 4"

Depth:
43' - 8"

Foundation:
CRAWLSPACE

Plan:
HPK1500039

Style:
TRADITIONAL

Square Footage:
1,557

Bedrooms:
3

Bathrooms:
2

Width:
46' - 0"

Depth:
40' - 0"

Foundation:
UNFINISHED WALKOUT BASEMENT

This split-foyer plan has the charm of a bungalow with its stone and shake facade. The visual impact is impressive as you stand in the foyer looking into the living and dining rooms, both voluminous with modified cathedral ceilings. The master suite features all the amenities of a large plan with separate tub and shower and double vanities. The oversized linen closet can convert to a washer/dryer closet if the ground-level location is not used. The third bath on the ground level allows for a fourth bedroom/rec room to be finished as the family grows. The best feture of this small home is the triple side-entrance garage. As with all split foyers, it can also be built with a front entry garage.

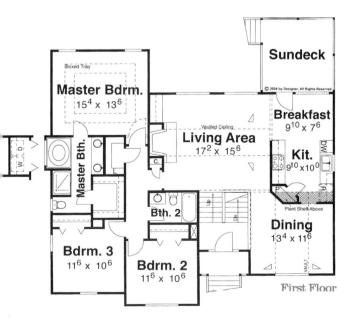

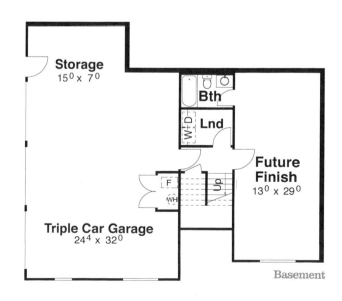

Plan:
HPK1500040

Style:
CRAFTSMAN

Square Footage:
1,644

Bedrooms:
3

Bathrooms:
2

Width:
34' - 0"

Depth:
68' - 0"

Foundation:
CRAWLSPACE, UNFINISHED WALKOUT BASEMENT

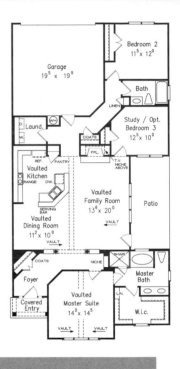

Plan:
HPK1500041

Style:
COUNTRY COTTAGE

Main Level:
1,273 SQ. FT.

Lower Level:
47 SQ. FT.

Total:
1,320 SQ. FT.

Bedrooms:
3

Bathrooms:
2

Width:
48' - 0"

Depth:
35' - 4"

Foundation:
UNFINISHED WALKOUT BASEMENT

Plan:
HPK1500042

Style:
COUNTRY COTTAGE

First Floor:
1,561 SQ. FT.

Second Floor:
578 SQ. FT.

Total:
2,139 SQ. FT.

Bonus Space:
284 SQ. FT.

Bedrooms:
3

Bathrooms:
2 ¹/₂

Width:
50' - 0"

Depth:
57' - 0"

Foundation:
CRAWLSPACE, FINISHED WALKOUT BASEMENT

Rear Exterior

Nostalgic and earthy, this Craftsman design has an attractive floor plan and thoughtful amenties. A column-lined covered porch is the perfect welcome to guests. A large vaulted family room, enhanced by a fireplace, opens to the spacious island kitchen and roomy breakfast area. The private master suite is embellished with a vaulted ceiling, walk-in closet, and vaulted super bath with French-door entry. With family in mind, two secondary bedrooms—each with a walk-in closet—share a computer workstation or loft area. A bonus room can be used as bedroom or home office.

First Floor

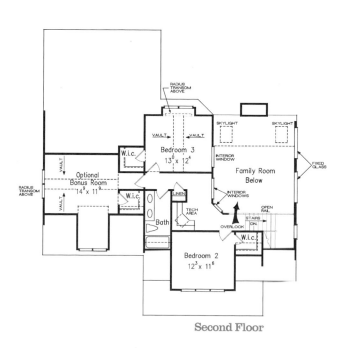

Second Floor

Plan:
HPK1500043

Style:
CRAFTSMAN

Square Footage:
1,997

Bonus Space:
310 SQ. FT.

Bedrooms:
3

Bathrooms:
2 ¹/₂

Width:
64' - 0"

Depth:
65' - 4"

Foundation:
UNFINISHED BASEMENT, CRAWLSPACE, SLAB

Rear Exterior

Plan:
HPK1500044

Style:
COUNTRY COTTAGE

Square Footage:
1,979

Bedrooms:
3

Bathrooms:
2

Width:
67' - 2"

Depth:
44' - 2"

Foundation:
UNFINISHED WALKOUT BASEMENT

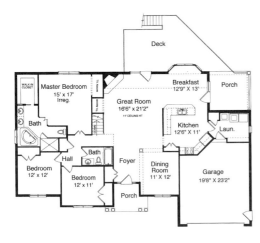

Plan:
HPK1500045

Style:
TRADITIONAL

Square Footage:
1,644

Bedrooms:
3

Bathrooms:
2

Width:
55' - 0"

Depth:
41' - 10"

Foundation:
SLAB

Plan:
HPK1500046

Style:	Total:	Width:
CRAFTSMAN	**2,410 SQ. FT.**	**46' - 0"**
First Floor:	Bonus Space:	Depth:
1,627 SQ. FT.	**418 SQ. FT.**	**58' - 0"**
Second Floor:	Bedrooms:	Foundation:
783 SQ. FT.	**4**	**CRAWLSPACE**
	Bathrooms:	
	2 ¹/₂	

First Floor

Second Floor

325 Summer Homes & Cottages
New Home Plans

Plan:
HPK1500047

Style:
COUNTRY COTTAGE

Main Level:
2,932 SQ. FT.

Lower Level:
1,556 SQ. FT.

Total:
4,488 SQ. FT.

Bedrooms:
3

Bathrooms:
3 1/2 + 1/2

Width:
114' - 0"

Depth:
83' - 0"

Foundation:
UNFINISHED WALKOUT BASEMENT

With a shingle and stone facade and rustic Craftsman touches, this country home will fit perfectly on a hill or mountainside. Designed to take advangtage of a glorious rear view, it both blends in with and celebrates its natural surroundings. The heart of the home is the enormous chimney with fireplaces on three sides including the master bedroom, the family room, and the covered terrace. Inside, massive trusses stretch above the kitchen and family room. These spaces connect seamlessly with the dining room. A decadent master suite resides on the main level, complete with two walk-in closets, a luxurious bath, and access to the covered terrace.

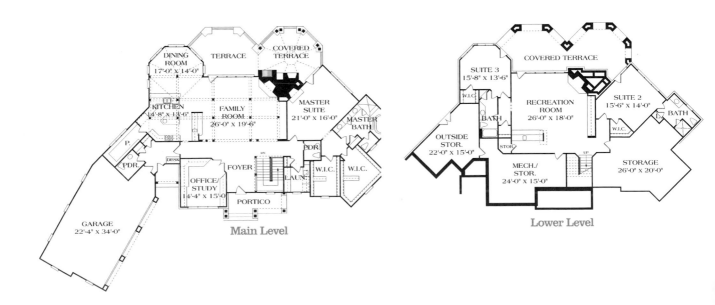

Main Level

Lower Level

BED #1
14' x 16'
9' Clg

SCREENED
PORCH
11' X 10'
9' Clg

DINING
15' x 10'-8"
11' Clg

LIVING
ROOM
18' x 18'
11' Clg

Slope

Eating
Bar

Slope

KIT
12'-8" x 10'

BED #2
12' x 11'-4"
9' Clg

D W

W.H.

Pantry

UP

Opt Bonus Rm
or Bsmt
Stairs

FOYER
9' Clg

BED #3
12' x 12'
9' Clg

GARAGE
23' x 21'

PATIO
10' Clg

OPT
GAME
ROOM
15' x 13'-4"

Slope
5' to 8'

1/2 Wall   DN

Attic

Plan:
HPK1500309

Style:
TRADITIONAL
Total:
1,812 SQ. FT.
Bonus Space:
210 SQ. FT.
Bedrooms:
3
Bathrooms:
2
Width:
46' - 0"
Depth:
65' - 0"

Plan:
HPK1500310

Style:	Bedrooms:	Width:
TRADITIONAL	**4**	**44' - 0"**
Square Footage:	Bathrooms:	Depth:
1,560	**2**	**58' - 0"**

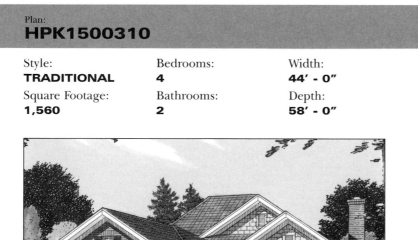

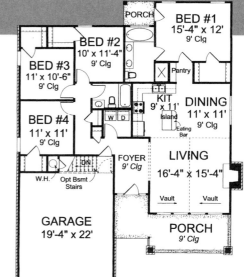

PORCH

BED #1
15'-4" x 12'
9' Clg

BED #2
10' x 11'-4"
9' Clg

BED #3
11' x 10'-6"
9' Clg

Pantry

KIT
9' x 11'
Island

DINING
11' x 11'
9' Clg

BED #4
11' x 11'
9' Clg

W D

Eating
Bar

DN

FOYER
9' Clg

LIVING
16'-4" x 15'-4"

W.H.

Opt Bsmt
Stairs

GARAGE
19'-4" x 22'

Vault   Vault

PORCH
9' Clg

Plan:
HPK1500048

Style:
TIDEWATER

First Floor:
1,314 SQ. FT.

Second Floor:
552 SQ. FT.

Total:
1,866 SQ. FT.

Bonus Space:
398 SQ. FT.

Bedrooms:
3

Bathrooms:
2 1/2

Width:
44' - 2"

Depth:
62' - 0"

Foundation:
CRAWLSPACE

© William E. Poole Designs, Inc.

First Floor

Second Floor

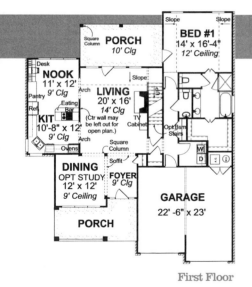

First Floor

Second Floor

Plan:
HPK1500049

Style:	Total:	Bathrooms:
FARMHOUSE	**1,977 SQ. FT.**	**2 1/2**
First Floor:	Bonus Space:	Width:
1,529 SQ. FT.	**292 SQ. FT.**	**49' - 0"**
Second Floor:	Bedrooms:	Depth:
448 SQ. FT.	**3**	**59' - 0"**

Plan:
HPK1500050

Style:
COUNTRY COTTAGE

Square Footage:
1,641

Bonus Space:
284 SQ. FT.

Bedrooms:
3

Bathrooms:
2

Width:
62' - 4"

Depth:
46' - 4"

Foundation:
UNFINISHED BASEMENT

A stone and siding exterior, covered porch, and multiple gable decorate the exterior of this popular one-level home. The interior offers a spacious great room with sloped ceiling, grand view to the rear yard, and charming fireplace. The adjoining dining area expands the living space for both a casual or more formal dining experience. A large kitchen with pantry and snack bar organizes the work area. The dramatic master bath with double bowl vanity, walk-in closet, separate shower enclosure, and large walk-in closet complement the master bedroom suite. A bonus space above the garage creates an area that can be used to best fit your family's needs. Two additional bedrooms and a full basement complete this wonderful home.

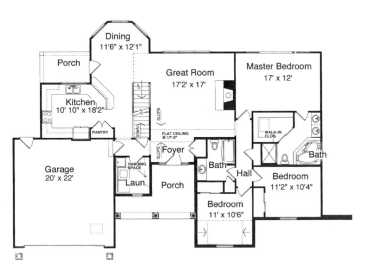

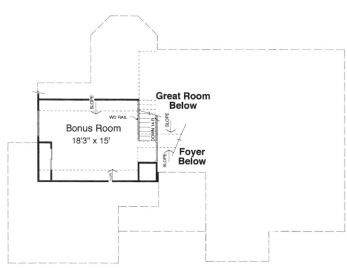

Plan:
HPK1500051

Style:
BUNGALOW

Square Footage:
1,444

Bedrooms:
3

Bathrooms:
2

Width:
49' - 6"

Depth:
52' - 4"

Foundation:
UNFINISHED BASEMENT

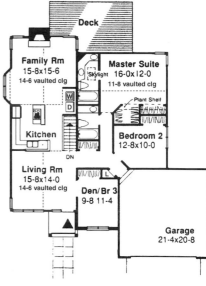

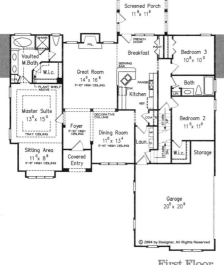

First Floor

Attic

Second Floor

Plan:
HPK1500052

Style:
COUNTRY COTTAGE

First Floor:
1,684 SQ. FT.

Second Floor:
279 SQ. FT.

Total:
1,963 SQ. FT.

Bedrooms:
4

Bathrooms:
3

Width:
53' - 0"

Depth:
67' - 4"

Foundation:
CRAWLSPACE, UNFINISHED WALKOUT BASEMENT, SLAB

Summer Homes & Cottages

325
New Home Plans

Plan:
HPK1500053

Style:
TRADITIONAL

Square Footage:
1,376

Bedrooms:
3

Bathrooms:
2

Width:
40' - 0"

Depth:
59' - 10"

Foundation:
SLAB

Alternate Exterior

Two exterior facades, one traditional and one country, enjoy subtle options like a living room bay window or a set of French doors to the front veranda. A fireplace enhances the living room and can be enjoyed from the dining room as well. The kitchen sports a walk-in pantry and patio access. Two family bedrooms share a full bath. The master suite features a large walk-in closet and private, compartmented bath.

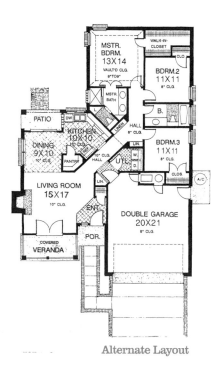

Alternate Layout

Plan:
HPK1500054

Style:
TRADITIONAL

Square Footage:
1,583

Bedrooms:
3

Bathrooms:
2

Width:
34' - 0"

Depth:
77' - 2"

© 2003 Donald A. Gardner, Inc.

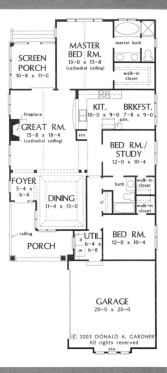

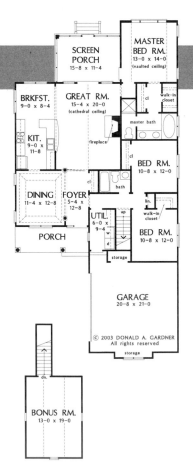

Plan:
HPK1500055

Style:
TRADITIONAL

Square Footage:
1,651

Bonus Space:
264 SQ. FT.

Bedrooms:
3

Bathrooms:
2

Width:
38' - 8"

Depth:
79' - 2"

© 2003 Donald A. Gardner, Inc.

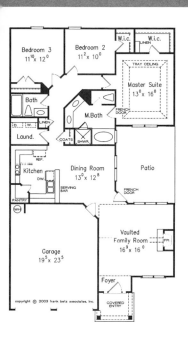

Plan:
HPK1500056

Style:
COUNTRY COTTAGE

Square Footage:
1,546

Bedrooms:
3

Bathrooms:
2

Width:
37' - 0"

Depth:
65' - 5"

Foundation:
SLAB

Plan:
HPK1500057

Style:	Bathrooms:	Foundation:
CRAFTSMAN	**2**	**CRAWLSPACE, UNFINISHED WALKOUT BASEMENT**
Square Footage:	Width:	
1,670	**34' - 0"**	
Bedrooms:	Depth:	
2	**77' - 0"**	

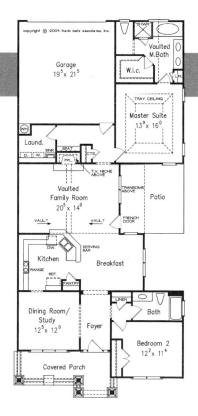

Plan: HPK1500058

Style:
CRAFTSMAN

Square Footage:
1,634

Bedrooms:
3

Bathrooms:
2

Width:
32' - 0"

Depth:
68' - 0"

Foundation:
CRAWLSPACE, UNFINISHED WALKOUT BASEMENT

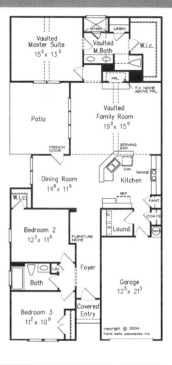

Optional Layout

Plan: HPK1500059

Style:
CRAFTSMAN

Square Footage:
1,502

Bedrooms:
2

Bathrooms:
2

Width:
32' - 0"

Depth:
67' - 8"

Foundation:
SLAB, UNFINISHED WALKOUT BASEMENT

Optional Layout

Summer Homes & Cottages

©2003 Donald A. Gardner, Inc.

BONUS RM.
15-0 x 22-0

Plan:
HPK1500060

Style:
TRADITIONAL

Square Footage:
1,614

Bonus Space:
410 SQ. FT.

Bedrooms:
3

Bathrooms:
2

Width:
52' - 11"

Depth:
54' - 2"

Plan:
HPK1500061

Style:
CRAFTSMAN

Square Footage:
1,949

Bonus Space:
416 SQ. FT.

Bedrooms:
3

Bathrooms:
2

Width:
56' - 4"

Depth:
64' - 0"

© 2003 DONALD A. GARDNER
All rights reserved

BONUS RM.
14-8 x 23-0

325 New Home Plans
Summer Homes & Cottages

Plan:
HPK1500062

Style:
COUNTRY COTTAGE

Square Footage:
1,406

Bedrooms:
3

Bathrooms:
2

Width:
50' - 4"

Depth:
49' - 0"

Foundation:
UNFINISHED WALKOUT BASEMENT, CRAWLSPACE, SLAB

This cozy country cottage boasts two covered porches, one in the front and one in the back. Inside, the foyer leads into the adjoining family room and dining room, both with vaulted ceilings and warmed by a centrally located fireplace. A pass-through from the kitchen allows convenient service to the dining room and an open flow for entertaining. The master suite dominates the right side of the plan complete with a tray ceiling in the bedroom, and a vaulted ceiling, dual vanities, a compartmented toilet, a separate shower, and a large walk-in closet in the bathroom. Two additional bedrooms share a full bath. A two-car garage completes this plan.

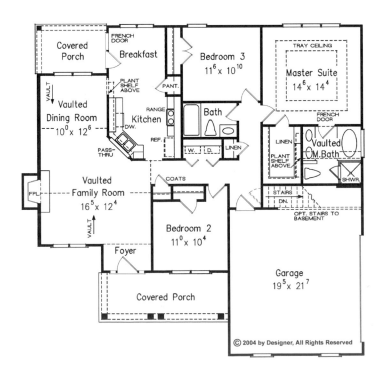

Summer Homes & Cottages

325 New Home Plans

Plan:
HPK1500063

Style:
TRADITIONAL

Square Footage:
1,737

Bonus Space:
299 SQ. FT.

Bedrooms:
3

Bathrooms:
2

Width:
54' - 4"

Depth:
54' - 10"

Foundation:
CRAWLSPACE

Plan:
HPK1500064

Style:
TRADITIONAL

Square Footage:
2,194

Bonus Space:
328 SQ. FT.

Bedrooms:
4

Bathrooms:
2

Width:
60' - 4"

Depth:
66' - 4"

Plan:
HPK1500311

Style:
COUNTRY COTTAGE

First Floor:
1,832 SQ. FT.

Second Floor:
574 SQ. FT.

Total:
2,406 SQ. FT.

Bonus Space:
410 SQ. FT.

Bedrooms:
4

Bathrooms:
3

Width:
77' - 10"

Depth:
41' - 4"

Foundation:
CRAWLSPACE

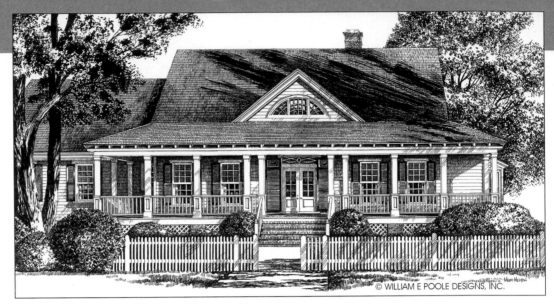

© WILLIAM E POOLE DESIGNS, INC.

This farmhouse style welcomes you with shuttered windows and doorway, and covered front and side porch. An open floor plan with an inside balcony creates a feeling of expansiveness. French doors; a gathering room with fireplace and access to the terrace; a kitchen with pantry, island, and breakfast nook; and everything the inhabitants of the master and one family bedroom will ever need round out the highlights of the main floor. Upstairs find bedrooms 3 and 4, a media center, and a great view to below.

First Floor

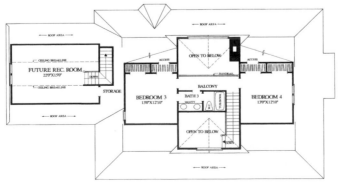

Second Floor

Plan:
HPK1500065

Style:
TRADITIONAL

Square Footage:
1,416

Bedrooms:
3

Bathrooms:
2

Width:
49' - 0"

Depth:
58' - 0"

BED #2
11' x 11'-6"
9' Ceiling

SCREEN PORCH
9'-8" x 12'

Slope

DINING
10' x 10'
10' Ceiling

LIVING
15' x 19'-6"
10' Ceiling

BED #1
12' x 15'
9' Ceiling

To Attic
(Opt Bsmt Stairs)

Eating Bar

BED #3
11' x 11'
9' Ceiling

KIT
11'-8"
x 10'-6"
Pantry

ENT
10' Clg

Stor

W D

PORCH
9' Ceiling

GARAGE
22' x 20'

Shop
7' x 8'

Plan:
HPK1500066

Style:
FARMHOUSE

Square Footage:
1,842

Bonus Space:
386 SQ. FT.

Bedrooms:
3

Bathrooms:
2

Width:
54' - 0"

Depth:
63' - 0"

MASTER BEDROOM
16' X 14'
9' CLG.

PORCH

VAULT

DINING
12'8" X 13'
12'CLG.

SCREEN PORCH
16' X 14'

PANTRY

REF

EATING BAR

PORCH

KITCHEN
14' X 13'
9'CLG.
ISLAND

LIVING ROOM
20' X 16'8"
12'CLG.

OVENS

DN

UP

BEDROOM 3
10' X 11'6"
9' CLG.

D W

LAUND.

TO ATTIC OR OPT.
GAMEROOM

OPTIONAL BASEMENT
STAIRS

GARAGE
20'4" X 22'

FOYER

OPT. DOORS

BEDROOM 2/
OPT. STUDY
11' X 12'4"
9'CLG.

PORCH

DN

OPTIONAL GAMEROOM
20'4" X 16'

Plan:
HPK1500067

Style:
COUNTRY COTTAGE

Square Footage:
1,573

Bonus Space:
276 SQ. FT.

Bedrooms:
3

Bathrooms:
2

Width:
50' - 0"

Depth:
57' - 8"

Foundation:
CRAWLSPACE, SLAB

This charming cottage design is a perfect second home or empty-nester. Two family bedrooms can be repurposed as an office and guest suite. A spacious kitchen overlooks the great room and breakfast area and is steps away from the formal dining room. A bonus room on the second floor can be used for storage or another guest suite.

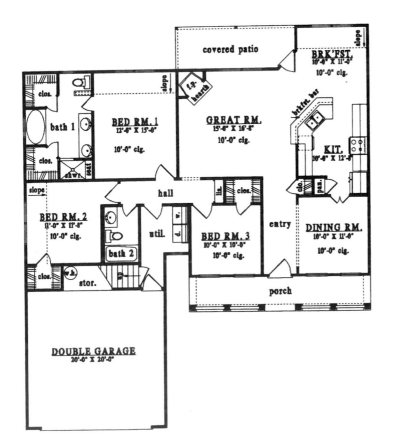

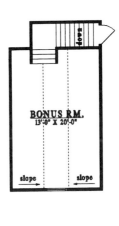

Plan:
HPK1500068

Style:
COUNTRY COTTAGE

First Floor:
2,357 SQ. FT.

Second Floor:
772 SQ. FT.

Total:
3,129 SQ. FT.

Bonus Space:
450 SQ. FT.

Bedrooms:
4

Bathrooms:
3

Width:
69' - 4"

Depth:
67' - 4"

Foundation:
CRAWLSPACE

© William E. Poole Designs, Inc.

Idyllic and uncompromising, this design exemplifies a country cottage with its use of triple dormers and a columned front porch. The living room is centrally located with a fireplace on the right wall and built-in bookcases. The island kitchen features a corner snack bar that serves the adjoining sunroom/breakfast area. A first-floor bedroom with full bath could serve as a guest suite or home office. The master suite, nestled in the far right corner of the first floor, is a quiet retreat for the homeowners. Upstairs, two family bedrooms share a full bath.

First Floor

© William E. Poole Designs

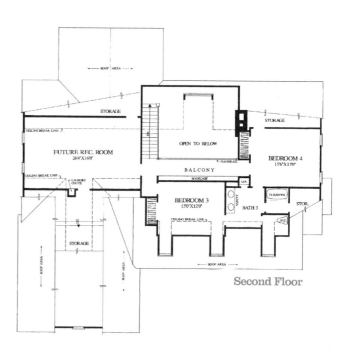

Second Floor

Plan:
HPK1500313

Style:
EUROPEAN COTTAGE

Square Footage:
1,612

Bedrooms:
2

Bathrooms:
2

Width:
42' - 0"

Depth:
67' - 4"

Foundation:
SLAB, UNFINISHED BASEMENT

Plan:
HPK1500312

Style:
EUROPEAN COTTAGE

Square Footage:
2,096 SQ. FT.

Bonus Space:
651 SQ. FT.

Bedrooms:
2

Bathrooms:
2

Width:
47' - 8"

Depth:
75' - 0"

Foundation:
SLAB, UNFINISHED BASEMENT

Plan:
HPK1500069

Style:
CRAFTSMAN

First Floor:
2,533 SQ. FT.

Second Floor:
1,820 SQ. FT.

Total:
4,353 SQ. FT.

Bonus Space:
507 SQ. FT.

Bedrooms:
4

Bathrooms:
3 ¹/2

Width:
85' - 10"

Depth:
81' - 6"

Foundation:
CRAWLSPACE

Take advantage of views on a hilly lot with this raised-foundation design. Craftsman touches outfit this home in rustic character but the floor plan keeps living spaces entirely modern. Four columns define the foyer and introduce the large gathering room. This space enjoys three sets of French doors, essentially opening the room to the outside. This open floor plan works magic in the kitchen, which serves up an island, pantry, and planning desk. A screened porch sits just off the spacious dining room. The first-floor master suite offers a place to relax. Three family suites, an open study nook, and bonus space makes room for everyone.

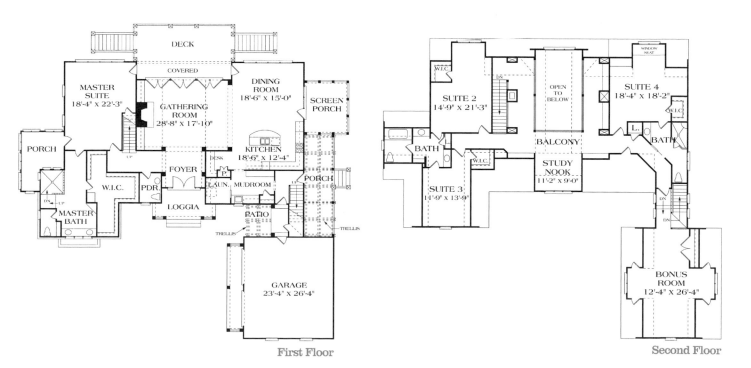

First Floor

Second Floor

Plan:
HPK1500070

Style:
COUNTRY COTTAGE

First Floor:
1,164 SQ. FT.

Second Floor:
1,319 SQ. FT.

Total:
2,483 SQ. FT.

Bedrooms:
4

Bathrooms:
3

Width:
50' - 0"

Depth:
39' - 0"

Foundation:
UNFINISHED WALKOUT BASEMENT

This charming cottage offers more space than you might think. A two-story living area is seen from the foyer where the U-shaped staircase leads you upstairs. The spacious kitchen/breakfast room even allows for a command center—the perfect place for the family computer. The first-floor bedroom provides space for an unexpected guest or can double as a home office. The master suite offers the option of a dramatic ceiling treatment with windows overlooking the rear of the house. A closet beyond the master bath makes room for all your clothes while also providing low storage. The other bedrooms also boast dramatic ceiling treatments, creating a sense of spaciousness.

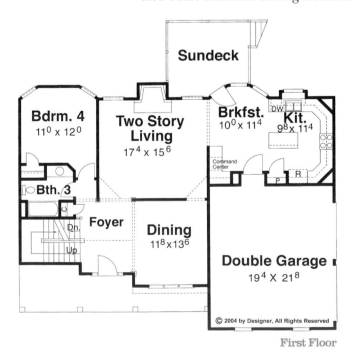

First Floor

Second Floor

Plan:
HPK1500071

Style:
CRAFTSMAN

First Floor:
2,218 SQ. FT.

Second Floor:
1,919 SQ. FT.

Total:
4,137 SQ. FT.

Bedrooms:
4

Bathrooms:
4

Width:
87' - 0"

Depth:
58' - 4"

Foundation:
CRAWLSPACE

A charming broken gable highlights the facade of this cottage design. The interior layout is perfect for empty-nesters who love to entertain or as a second home near the lake. Decorative columns set off the dining room and gathering room, dressing up this more formal spaces. The gourmet kitchen has plenty of room for two or more chefs and is built to entertain talkitive guests. The breakfast room enjoys a bank of windows and access to the screened porch. A guest room would make a perfect den or home office. Relax in the first-floor master suite outfitted with porch access, twin walk-in closets, and a super bath. For guests and family, the second level has two suites, an office—or bedroom—bonus room, library, and home theater.

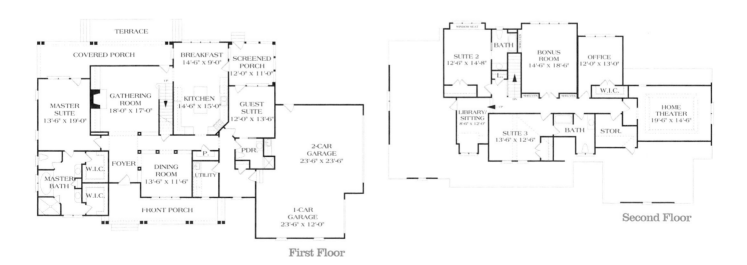

First Floor

Second Floor

Plan:
HPK1500072

Style:
COUNTRY COTTAGE

First Floor:
1,315 SQ. FT.

Second Floor:
1,380 SQ. FT.

Total:
2,695 SQ. FT.

Bedrooms:
5

Bathrooms:
3

Width:
50' - 0"

Depth:
44' - 0"

Foundation:
UNFINISHED WALKOUT BASEMENT

This plan says "welcome home," as Craftsman details make a warm entry. The view from the front door to the family room's two-story fireplace wall is amazing. The garage entry brings you past a home office, which can easily be used as a guest bedroom. The expansive kitchen/breakfast area also features a command center—perfect for the family computer. A staircase leads to the second-floor balcony where three bedrooms share a bath. The master suite features a window seat on the back wall, dramatized by a stepped ceiling and large windows overlooking the back yard. An oversized master closet even has extra storage space that could be cedar-lined for those out-of-season clothes. The second-floor laundry and computer desk complete this well-appointed design.

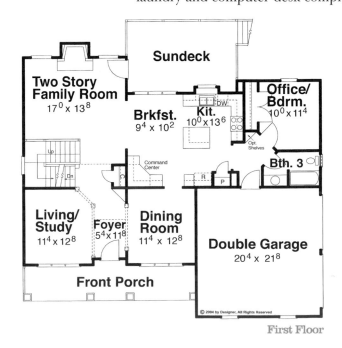

First Floor

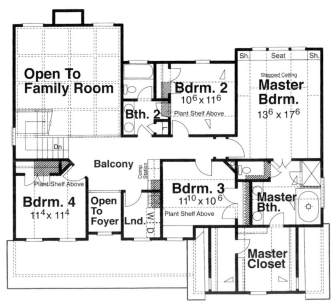

Second Floor

Plan:
HPK1500314

Style:
TRADITIONAL

First Floor:
1,619 SQ. FT.

Second Floor:
372 SQ. FT.

Total:
1,991 SQ. FT.

Bonus Space:
82 SQ. FT.

Bedrooms:
3

Bathrooms:
3

Width:
46' - 8"

Depth:
70' - 8"

Euro-French Country traditional sums up this exquisite hideaway. A complex roof line enhances rustic exteriors and a chimney sure to charm! Cathedral-style ceilings adorn the main level. Enter your home and be greeted by a fireplace in the foyer on your immediate right, and a den on the left. Continue straight ahead to the great room, where you can view your enclosed deck, and access your kitchen with accompanying eating area. A master suite with walk-in closet is to the right of the kitchen. A second bathroom and the garage are accessed through the kitchen as well. Upstairs you will find plenty to do, including an office with built-in desk, and an extra kitchen!

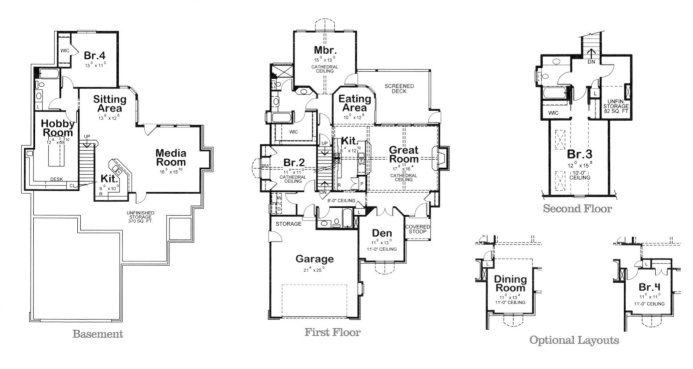

Basement

First Floor

Second Floor

Optional Layouts

Plan:
HPK1500073

Style:
CRAFTSMAN

Square Footage:
2,326

Bonus Space:
358 SQ. FT.

Bedrooms:
3

Bathrooms:
2 1/2

Width:
64' - 0"

Depth:
72' - 4"

Foundation:
FINISHED BASEMENT

Plan:
HPK1500074

Style:
CRAFTSMAN

Square Footage:
2,326

Bonus Space:
358 SQ. FT.

Bedrooms:
3

Bathrooms:
2 1/2

Width:
64' - 0"

Depth:
72' - 4"

Foundation:
FINISHED WALKOUT BASEMENT

Plan:
HPK1500075

Style:
COUNTRY COTTAGE

First Floor:
2,499 SQ. FT.

Second Floor:
1,130 SQ. FT.

Total:
3,629 SQ. FT.

Bedrooms:
5

Bathrooms:
4

Width:
67' - 6"

Depth:
69' - 10"

Foundation:
CRAWLSPACE, UNFINISHED WALKOUT BASEMENT, SLAB

Alluring details; four embellished dormers and stone-and-brick materials give this home curb appeal. A formal foyer and dining room view the covered front porch. To the rear, the family room enhanced by a coffered ceiling, built-ins, a bank of windows, and a fireplace is the perfect spot to entertain. For causal times, the keeping room, breakfast space, island kitchen, and screened porch will be the most used area of the home. The master suite provides a sitting bay, super bath, and large walk-in closet. A vaulted home office sits right across the hall. Two family bedrooms share a compartmented bath, media desk, and a bonus retreat.

First Floor

Second Floor

Plan:
HPK1500076

Style:
FARMHOUSE

Square Footage:
2,326

Bonus Space:
358 SQ. FT.

Bedrooms:
3

Bathrooms:
2 ¹/₂

Width:
64' - 0"

Depth:
72' - 4"

Foundation:
FINISHED WALKOUT BASEMENT

Plan:
HPK1500077

Style:
CRAFTSMAN

First Floor:
1,799 SQ. FT.

Second Floor:
709 SQ. FT.

Total:
2,508 SQ. FT.

Bonus Space:
384 SQ. FT.

Bedrooms:
3

Bathrooms:
2 ¹/₂

Width:
77' - 4"

Depth:
41' - 4"

Foundation:
UNFINISHED WALKOUT BASEMENT

First Floor

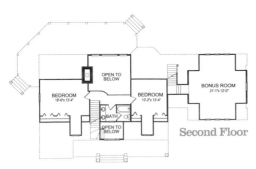

Second Floor

325
New Home Plans

Plan:
HPK1500078

Style:
COUNTRY COTTAGE

First Floor:
1,845 SQ. FT.

Second Floor:
799 SQ. FT.

Total:
2,644 SQ. FT.

Bedrooms:
4

Bathrooms:
3

Width:
61' - 0"

Depth:
57' - 4"

Foundation:
CRAWLSPACE, UNFINISHED WALKOUT BASEMENT, SLAB

Centered windows on front-facing gables perch atop a Craftsman-style porch creating a delightful neighborhood home. The uncluttered layout takes advantage of its space by opening up the casual living areas. A vaulted family room features a fireplace with sidelights and an uninterrupted view of the breakfast space and island kitchen. Enjoy three seasons of alfresco dining on the screened porch. The first-floor master suite is enhanced by a tray ceiling and super bath. Across the hall, a home office looks out to the front yard. Additional bedrooms are placed on the second level, and each sports a walk-in closet and has access to the vaulted loft.

First Floor

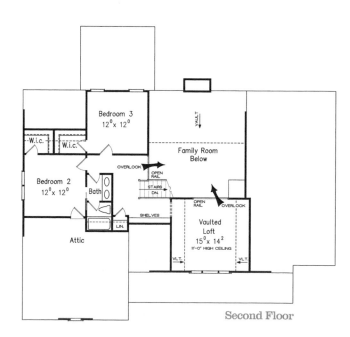

Second Floor

Plan:
HPK1500079

Style:
CRAFTSMAN

First Floor:
1,799 SQ. FT.

Second Floor:
709 SQ. FT.

Total:
2,508 SQ. FT.

Bonus Space:
384 SQ. FT.

Bedrooms:
3

Bathrooms:
2 1/2

Width:
77' - 4"

Depth:
41' - 4"

Foundation:
UNFINISHED WALKOUT BASEMENT

First Floor

Second Floor

Plan:
HPK1500080

Style:
CRAFTSMAN

First Floor:
1,799 SQ. FT.

Second Floor:
709 SQ. FT.

Total:
2,508 SQ. FT.

Bonus Space:
384 SQ. FT.

Bedrooms:
3

Bathrooms:
2 1/2

Width:
77' - 4"

Depth:
41' - 4"

Foundation:
UNFINISHED WALKOUT BASEMENT

First Floor

Second Floor

Rustic Getaways & Retreats

Plan:
HPK1500081

Style:
COUNTRY COTTAGE

First Floor:
1,755 SQ. FT.

Second Floor:
864 SQ. FT.

Total:
2,619 SQ. FT.

Bedrooms:
4

Bathrooms:
3 ¹/₂

Width:
56' - 0"

Depth:
53' - 0"

Foundation:
CRAWLSPACE, UNFINISHED WALKOUT BASEMENT, SLAB

Comfortable and modern great room design caters to the active family that requires more active space than formal spaces. The island kitchen will be a favorite hang out for everyone. A formal dining room is a great area for entertaining and enjoying the holiday meals. A first-floor master suite inlcudes a amenity-filled bath and walk-in closet. Upstairs, three secondary bedrooms share two full baths.

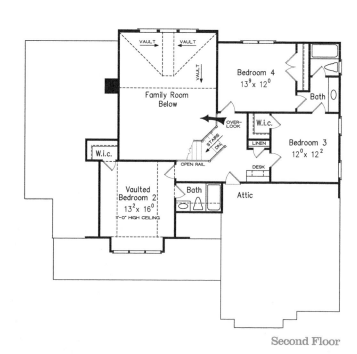

First Floor

Second Floor

Plan:
HPK1500082

Style:
COUNTRY COTTAGE

First Floor:
2,589 SQ. FT.

Second Floor:
981 SQ. FT.

Total:
3,570 SQ. FT.

Bedrooms:
4

Bathrooms:
3 1/2

Width:
70' - 8"

Depth:
61' - 10"

Foundation:
CRAWLSPACE

First Floor

Second Floor

Plan:
HPK1500083

Style:
FARMHOUSE

First Floor:
2,589 SQ. FT.

Second Floor:
981 SQ. FT.

Total:
3,570 SQ. FT.

Bedrooms:
4

Bathrooms:
3 1/2

Width:
70' - 8"

Depth:
61' - 10"

Foundation:
CRAWLSPACE

First Floor

Second Floor

ORDER BLUEPRINTS 24 HOURS, 7 DAYS A WEEK, AT 1-800-521-6797 OR EPLANS.COM

Rustic Getaways & Retreats

Plan:
HPK1500084

Style:
CRAFTSMAN

First Floor:
941 SQ. FT.

Second Floor:
786 SQ. FT.

Total:
1,727 SQ. FT.

Bedrooms:
3

Bathrooms:
2 ½

Width:
57' - 10"

Depth:
42' - 4"

Foundation:
UNFINISHED BASEMENT

A stone-and-siding exterior brings dimension and color to this charming home. A two-story foyer greets you upon arrival, and the great room, with views to the rear and side yards, offers a 12-foot ceiling. The breakfast bay and entry to a covered porch create a bright and cheery place to start the day. Counter space that wraps around from the kitchen provides additional storage and a convenient writing desk. A furniture alcove adds space to the formal dining room and a rear entry hall offers storage closets and a large laundry room. A second-floor master bedroom, with a ceiling that slopes to nine feet, keeps the parents close at hand to younger family members. This home has a full basement that can be developed for additional square footage.

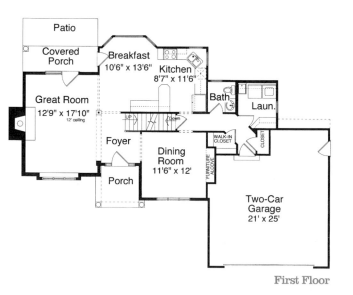

First Floor

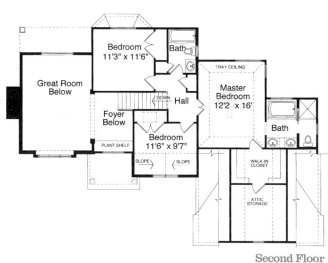

Second Floor

Plan:
HPK1500315

Style:
CRAFTSMAN

Square Footage:
1,899

Bedrooms:
2

Bathrooms:
2 ¹/₂

Width:
62' - 0"

Depth:
68' - 8"

A hipped dormer on the exterior and a tray ceiling inside provide highlights to the dining room of this traditional Craftsman home. Escape to the privacy of your master suite and its own whirlpool tub (four extra bathrooms throughout the house means no sharing!). The kitchen is tucked away from traffic, but within view of the amply spaced eating area. The main floor of this house has an additional covered porch in the rear corner leading off of the garage. Both the den and family bedroom feature built-in desks. These conveniences are mirrored upstairs with a ready-to-use bookcase, hutch, wine storage, and bar. Entertain upstairs in style, and still have plenty of space available for all of your storage needs.

First Floor

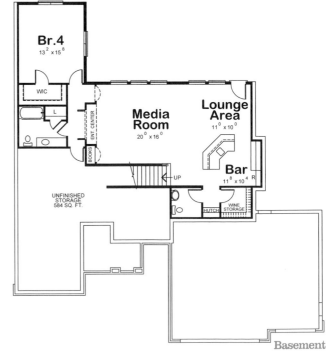

Basement

Plan:
HPK1500085

Style:
CRAFTSMAN

First Floor:
2,896 SQ. FT.

Second Floor:
986 SQ. FT.

Total:
3,882 SQ. FT.

Bonus Space:
480 SQ. FT.

Bedrooms:
4

Bathrooms:
3 ¹/₂

Width:
76' - 11"

Depth:
101' - 7"

Foundation:
CRAWLSPACE

Perfect winter getaway home! This retreat includes all the comforts of home: formal dining area, private study, cozy living room, gourmet kitchen, and open family room. The quiet master suite will relax and pamper the homeowner with a large super bath, dual walk-in closets, and French doors to the deck. The second level gives the family privacy with three bedrooms and two full baths. Above the garage, a bonus room will make comfortable guest quarters.

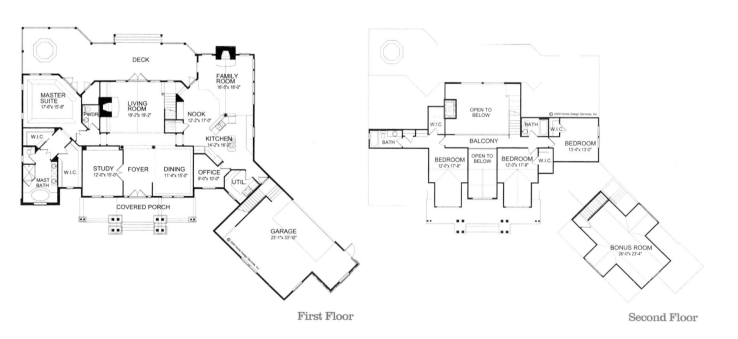

First Floor

Second Floor

325
New Home Plans

Rustic Getaways & Retreats

Plan:
HPK1500086

Style:
CRAFTSMAN

First Floor:
2,896 SQ. FT.

Second Floor:
986 SQ. FT.

Total:
3,882 SQ. FT.

Bonus Space:
480 SQ. FT.

Bedrooms:
4

Bathrooms:
3 ¹/₂

Width:
76' - 11"

Depth:
101' - 7"

Foundation:
CRAWLSPACE

Stone and wood siding, borrowed from nature, give this home design a woodsy resort style. Windows, transoms, and French doors allow plenty of light and the surrounding view to fill the home. A spacious foyer introduces the dining room and private study. To the rear, the great room is outfitted with a fireplace, built-ins, and an expansive deck just beyond French doors. A trio of warm casual spaces—the oversized kitchen, eating nook, and family room—creates an incredibly livable combination. A home office is tucked behind the kitchen for privacy. Three secondary bedrooms are positioned upstairs, giving the master suite plenty of seclusion on the first floor.

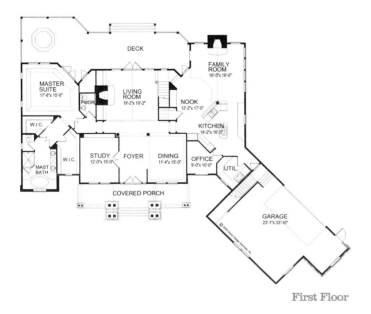

First Floor

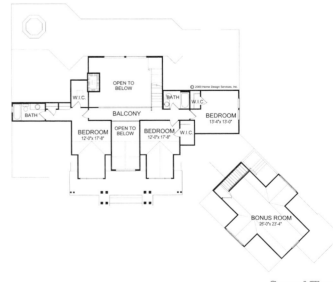

Second Floor

84

ORDER BLUEPRINTS 24 HOURS, 7 DAYS A WEEK, AT 1-800-521-6797 OR EPLANS.COM

Rustic Getaways & Retreats

325 New Home Plans

Plan:
HPK1500087

Style:
CRAFTSMAN

First Floor:
2,896 SQ. FT.

Second Floor:
986 SQ. FT.

Total:
3,882 SQ. FT.

Bonus Space:
480 SQ. FT.

Bedrooms:
4

Bathrooms:
3 1/2

Width:
76' - 11"

Depth:
101' - 7"

Foundation:
CRAWLSPACE

Dream of living in a log cabin? Embrace that dream with this Craftsman-detailed log cabin home and start living in rustic refinement. A formal study and dining room flank the foyer. An open and expansive living room features a fireplace and French doors to the deck. The master suite enjoys seclusion on the first floor and is complete with walk-in closets and full bath. The outstanding combination of kitchen, eating nook, and family room caters to the busy family who likes casual entertaining of friends. Upstairs, three secondary bedrooms all have walk-in closets and share two full baths. A bonus room above the garage can be converted to guest quarters.

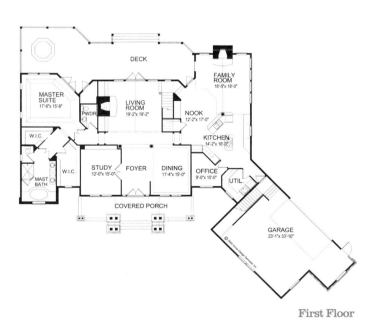

First Floor

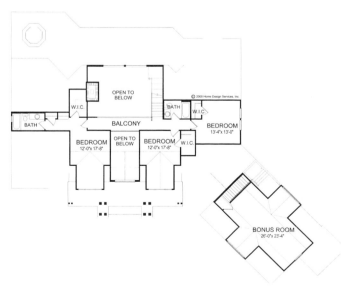

Second Floor

Plan:
HPK1500088

Style:
FARMHOUSE

Square Footage:
1,298

Bedrooms:
3

Bathrooms:
2

Width:
48' - 6"

Depth:
36' - 0"

Foundation:
CRAWLSPACE, UNFINISHED BASEMENT

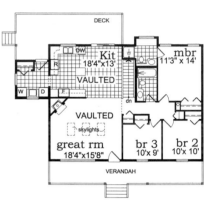

Plan:
HPK1500089

Style:
FARMHOUSE

Square Footage:
1,092

Width:
46' - 0"

Bedrooms:
3

Bathrooms:
1

Depth:
32' - 0"

Foundation:
CRAWLSPACE, SLAB

325
New Home Plans

Plan:
HPK1500090

Style:
FARMHOUSE

Square Footage:
1,514

Bedrooms:
3

Bathrooms:
2

Width:
63' - 0"

Depth:
40' - 0"

Foundation:
CRAWLSPACE, UNFINISHED BASEMENT

Plan:
HPK1500091

Style:
FARMHOUSE

Square Footage:
1,455

Bedrooms:
3

Bathrooms:
2

Width:
50' - 6"

Depth:
38' - 0"

Foundation:
CRAWLSPACE, UNFINISHED BASEMENT

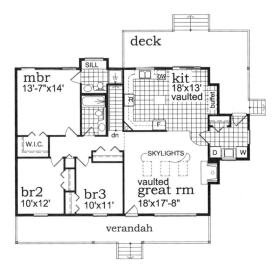

Plan:
HPK1500092

Style:
FARMHOUSE

Square Footage:
1,601

Bedrooms:
3

Bathrooms:
2

Width:
60' - 0"

Depth:
44' - 0"

Foundation:
CRAWLSPACE, UNFINISHED BASEMENT

A beautiful wraparound porch takes full advantage of 360-degree views. This country home also offers a striking breakfast bay to the rear. Formal spaces, the living and dining rooms, are positioned near the front with plenty of windows, a fireplace, and French doors to the porch. The nearby kitchen includes a small island for quick food preparation, a pantry, a laundry closet, and a bright adjoining breakfast space. The master suite enjoys French doors to the porch and a private bath. Two family bedrooms share a full bath.

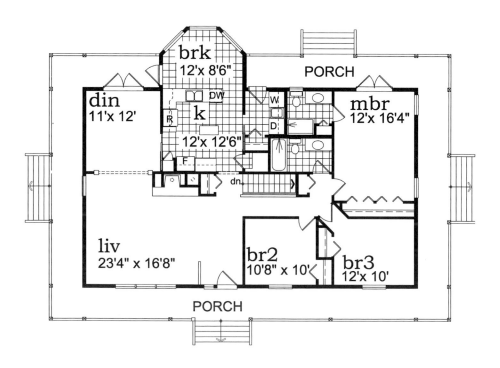

325
New Home Plans

First Floor

Second Floor

Plan:
HPK1500093

Style:
CONTEMPORARY

First Floor:
1,108 SQ. FT.

Second Floor:
517 SQ. FT.

Total:
1,625 SQ. FT.

Bedrooms:
3

Bathrooms:
2

Width:
36' - 0"

Depth:
36' - 0"

Foundation:
UNFINISHED BASEMENT

Plan:
HPK1500094

Style:
EUROPEAN COTTAGE

First Floor:
780 SQ. FT.

Second Floor:
600 SQ. FT.

TOTAL:
1,380 sq. ft.

BEDROOMS:
3

BATHROOMS:
2

WIDTH:
26' - 0"

DEPTH:
30' - 0"

Foundation:
UNFINISHED BASEMENT

First Floor

Second Floor

Plan:
HPK1500095

Style:
CONTEMPORARY

First Floor:
784 SQ. FT.

Second Floor:
597 SQ. FT.

Total:
1,381 SQ. FT.

Bedrooms:
3

Bathrooms:
1 ¹/₂

Width:
28' - 0"

Depth:
28' - 0"

Foundation:
UNFINISHED BASEMENT

A wraparound deck is a great stargazing site on dark forest nights. This cottage sports an enclosed porch for cooler evenings and a mud room with a walk-in closet for heavy coats. The island kitchen also serves as a casual meal space while the more formal dining area is ideal for larger get togethers. Upstairs, three bedrooms share a main bath.

First Floor

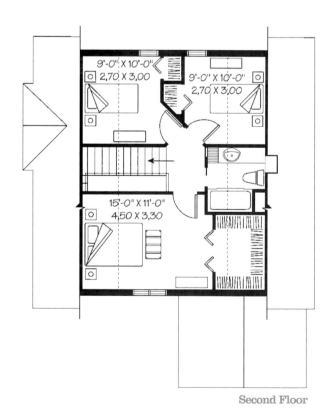

Second Floor

Plan:
HPK1500096

Style:
LAKEFRONT

Square Footage:
1,114

Bedrooms:
2

Bathrooms:
1

Width:
39' - 8"

Depth:
36' - 4"

Foundation:
**UNFINISHED
BASEMENT**

Lakeside or curbside, this 1,114-square-foot design soars to new heights for relaxed living. A second-story portico and walls of light-loving windows surround the exterior. The master bedroom with full bath, and family room with fireplace enjoy a lofty cathedral ceiling. A spacious second bedroom, rounded kitchen with sprawling lunch counter, and gracious dining room complement this outstanding space.

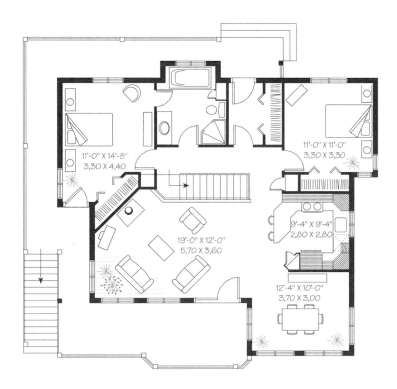

Plan:
HPK1500097

Style:
LAKEFRONT

First Floor:
967 SQ. FT.

Second Floor:
1,076 SQ. FT.

Third Floor:
349 SQ. FT.

Total:
2,392 SQ. FT.

Bedrooms:
5

Bathrooms:
3 ½

Width:
39′ - 8″

Depth:
36′ - 8″

Foundation:
PIER (SAME AS PILING)

Three levels of beach living at its finest! From the shore this house will stand out with its spectacular porches, balconies, and staircases. Starting from the top you'll find a guest room with its own bathroom, secluded for privacy. The second level holds a kitchen with an island for informal meals and a dining room for more formal entertaining occasions. The dining room and family room both enjoy access to a balcony. The master suite is also on this level and includes an expansive closet leading to the master bath. Three more bedrooms, a full bath, and the living room occupy the first level, along with a laundry room—necessary for keeping beach clothes sand-free.

First Floor

Second Floor

Third Floor

Plan:
HPK1500329

Style:
TRADITIONAL

Square Footage:
2,176

Basement:
957 SQ. FT.

Bedrooms:
2

Bathrooms.
2

Width:
70' - 8"

Depth:
68' - 8"

Brick with window shutters on the outside lends old-fashioned appeal to this plan. Inside, the great room serves as the focal point, located directly off the foyer. Windows looking out to the rear frame a fireplace, and an arch separates the dining room. The kitchen area is easily accessible from the great room, and is built for all of your food storage, serving and preparation needs. The dining room offers access onto the deck (covered!) and to the second bedroom and to the study. The kitchen offers access to the garage with shop. The master bedroom is accessed via double doors from the great room, and comes with a luxurious bath and incredible walk-in closet. Upstairs is the third bedroom with private bath and separate dressing area, family room, rec room, and storage.

Plan:
HPK1500098

Style:
EUROPEAN COTTAGE

Square Footage:
1,648

Bedrooms:
3

Bathrooms:
2

Width:
40' - 0"

Depth:
66' - 8"

Foundation:
SLAB

First Floor

Plan:
HPK1500099

Style:
COUNTRY COTTAGE

First Floor:
1,774 SQ. FT.

Second Floor:
525 SQ. FT.

Total:
2,299 SQ. FT.

Bonus Space:
300 SQ. FT.

Bedrooms:
4

Bathrooms:
3

Width:
56' - 0"

Depth:
63' - 4"

Foundation:
CRAWLSPACE, UNFINISHED WALKOUT BASEMENT, SLAB

Second Floor

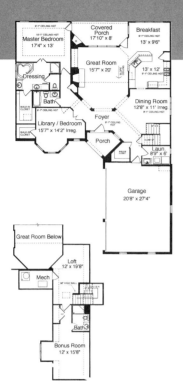

Plan:
HPK1500316

Style:
EUROPEAN COTTAGE

Square Footage:
1,953

Bonus Space:
652 SQ. FT.

Bedrooms:
3

Bathrooms:
3

Width:
50' - 0"

Depth:
75' - 0"

Foundation:
SLAB, UNFINISHED BASEMENT

Plan:
HPK1500100

Style:	Bedrooms:	Depth:
FRENCH	**3**	**68' - 1"**
Square Footage:	Bathrooms:	Foundation:
2,904	**2 1/2**	**FINISHED**
Basement:	Width:	**WALKOUT**
1,905 SQ. FT.	**76' - 0"**	**BASEMENT**

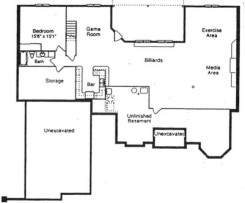

Plan:
HPK1500101

Style:
COLONIAL

Square Footage:
1,704

Bonus Space:
364 SQ. FT.

Bedrooms:
3

Bathrooms:
2 ¹/₂

Width:
71' - 0"

Depth:
50' - 0"

Foundation:
CRAWLSPACE, SLAB

Plan:
HPK1500102

Style:
TRADITIONAL

Square Footage:
1,452

Bedrooms:
3

Bathrooms:
2

Width:
55' - 0"

Depth:
40' - 10"

Foundation:
SLAB

Alternate Exterior

Plan:
HPK1500103

Style:
FARMHOUSE

First Floor:
902 SQ. FT.

Second Floor:
1,147 SQ. FT.

Total:
2,049 SQ. FT.

Bedrooms:
4

Bathrooms:
2 ½

Width:
52' - 0"

Depth:
36' - 4"

Foundation:
UNFINISHED BASEMENT

Brick facing, narrow footprint, and a set-back two-car garage make this farmhouse design a perfect in-fill home. A livable floor plan includes a formal entry flanked by a library and powder room. To the rear, a roomy great room sports a fireplace, which can be enjoyed from the dining room and kitchen. Upstairs, three family bedrooms features big closets and share a hall bath. The master suite is outfitted with a walk-in closet and a private full bath with dual-sink vanity.

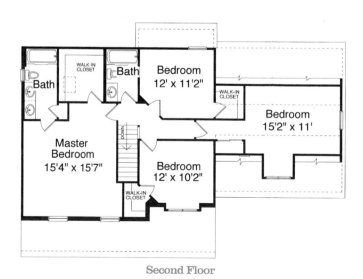

First Floor

Second Floor

Plan:
HPK1500104

Style:
TRADITIONAL

Square Footage:
2,061

Bedrooms:
3

Bathrooms:
3

Width:
70' - 0"

Depth:
52' - 0"

Foundation:
CRAWLSPACE, SLAB, UNFINISHED BASEMENT

Optional Layout

Plan:
HPK1500105

Style:
COUNTRY COTTAGE

Square Footage:
1,492

Bedrooms:
3

Bathrooms:
2

Width:
56' - 0"

Depth:
45' - 8"

Foundation:
CRAWLSPACE, SLAB, UNFINISHED BASEMENT

Optional Layout

Plan:
HPK1500106

Style:
TRADITIONAL

Square Footage:
2,775

Bonus Space:
1,606 SQ. FT.

Bedrooms:
3

Bathrooms:
2 ¹/₂

Width:
74' - 0"

Depth:
53' - 10"

Foundation:
FINISHED WALKOUT BASEMENT

First Floor

Basement

Plan:
HPK1500107

Style:
FARMHOUSE

Square Footage:
1,604

Bonus Space:
316 SQ. FT.

Bedrooms:
3

Bathrooms:
2

Width:
57' - 0"

Depth:
59' - 0"

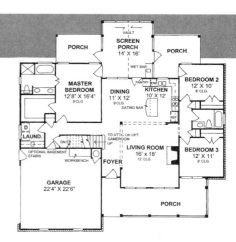

Optional Layout

Plan:
HPK1500108

Style:
COUNTRY COTTAGE

Square Footage:
2,078

Bedrooms:
3

Bathrooms:
2

Width:
62' - 8"

Depth:
57' - 11"

Foundation:
UNFINISHED WALKOUT BASEMENT

Plan:
HPK1500109

Style:
COUNTRY COTTAGE

Square Footage:
1,751

Bedrooms:
3

Bathrooms:
2

Width:
62' - 8"

Depth:
42' - 2"

Foundation:
UNFINISHED WALKOUT BASEMENT

Plan:

HPK1500110

Style:
FARMHOUSE

First Floor:
1,107 SQ. FT.

Second Floor:
1,243 SQ. FT.

Total:
2,350 SQ. FT.

Bedrooms:
3

Bathrooms:
2 ¹/₂

Width:
58' - 0"

Depth:
33' - 0"

Foundation:
UNFINISHED BASEMENT

Take one look at this traditional home and you'll know: a love of the outdoors is essential for those living inside. An expansive porch hugs nearly the entire first level, and the second level, not to be outdone, includes a balcony accessed by the master suite and sitting area! The snack-bar kitchen points to the formal dining room to its right and straight ahead to a half-bath and laundry room. A spacious living room includes a fireplace. Two more bedrooms upstairs share a full hall bath.

First Floor

Second Floor

Plan:
HPK1500111

Style:
COUNTRY COTTAGE

Square Footage:
2,439

Bonus Space:
390 SQ. FT.

Bedrooms:
3

Bathrooms:
2 1/2

Width:
77' - 0"

Depth:
59' - 1"

Foundation:
CRAWLSPACE, SLAB

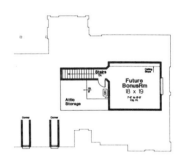

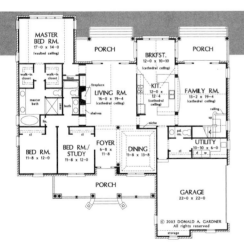

Plan:
HPK1500112

Style:
TRADITIONAL

Square Footage:
2,639

Bonus Space:
425 SQ. FT.

Bedrooms:
3

Bathrooms:
2 1/2

Width:
67' - 3"

Depth:
69' - 9"

Plan:
HPK1500113

Style:
CONTEMPORARY

First Floor:
1,232 SQ. FT.

Second Floor:
951 SQ. FT.

Total:
2,183 SQ. FT.

Bonus Space:
365 SQ. FT.

Bedrooms:
3

Bathrooms:
2 1/2

Width:
56' - 4"

Depth:
44' - 0"

Foundation:
UNFINISHED BASEMENT

The brick exterior provides a strong and attractive appeal to the facade of this traditional design. A cozy family room is tucked into the front right corner of the plan, right next to the foyer with a coat closet. The living room to the left includes a corner fireplace and access to the solarium. The L-shaped kitchen has a convenient island—perfect for extra counter space or as an informal eating area—and flows into the breakfast nook. Sleeping areas are found on the second floor. Two family bedrooms have abundant closets and share a full hall bath. The master suite is a study in luxury with its enormous walk-in closet and pampering bath, complete with separate corner tub and shower, compartmented toilet, and a dual-sink vanity. Turn the bonus space into a home theater or an extra bedroom at your leisure.

First Floor

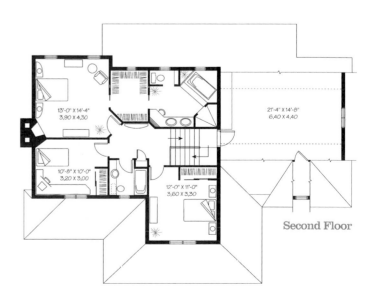

Second Floor

Plan:
HPK1500114

Style:
FARMHOUSE

First Floor:
1,736 SQ. FT.

Second Floor:
516 SQ. FT.

Total:
2,252 SQ. FT.

Bonus Space:
272 SQ. FT.

Bedrooms:
4

Bathrooms:
3

Width:
80' - 0"

Depth:
59' - 0"

First Floor

Second Floor

First Floor

Plan:
HPK1500115

Style:
CONTEMPORARY

First Floor:
1,060 SQ. FT.

Second Floor:
1,039 SQ. FT.

Total:
2,099 SQ. FT.

Bedrooms:
4

Bathrooms:
2 1/2

Width:
50' - 0"

Depth:
39' - 0"

Foundation:
UNFINISHED BASEMENT

Second Floor

Plan:
HPK1500116

Style:
CONTEMPORARY

First Floor:
1,222 SQ. FT.

Second Floor:
1,134 SQ. FT.

Total:
2,356 SQ. FT.

Bedrooms:
4

Bathrooms:
2 ¹/2

Width:
54' - 0"

Depth:
45' - 0"

Foundation:
UNFINISHED BASEMENT

A traditional plan offers a sensible layout as well as sophisticated touches. On the first floor, the dine-in kitchen and sun room establish enjoyable gathering spaces for family dinners and other informal occasions. Families will also appreciate the hard-working mud room and half-bath at the left of the plan, above the spacious garage. Formal dining and living spaces surround the pleasing entry foyer.

This home, as shown in photographs, may differ from the actual blueprints. For more detailed information, please check the floor plans carefully.

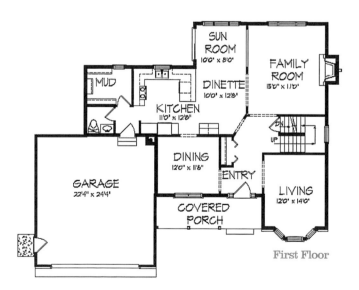

First Floor

Second Floor

Plan:
HPK1500117

Style:
CONTEMPORARY

First Floor:
1,371 SQ. FT.

Second Floor:
894 SQ. FT.

Total:
2,265 SQ. FT.

Bonus Space:
339 SQ. FT.

Bedrooms:
4

Bathrooms:
3 1/2

Width:
58' - 0"

Depth:
58' - 4"

Foundation:
UNFINISHED BASEMENT

First Floor

Second Floor

Plan:
HPK1500118

Style:
CONTEMPORARY

First Floor:
1,044 SQ. FT.

Second Floor:
892 SQ. FT.

Total:
1,936 SQ. FT.

Bonus Space:
289 SQ. FT.

Bedrooms:
3

Bathrooms:
2 1/2

Width:
58' - 0"

Depth:
43' - 6"

Foundation:
UNFINISHED BASEMENT

First Floor

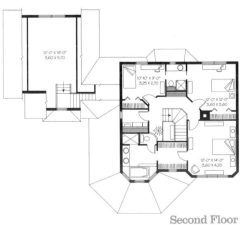

Second Floor

First Floor

Second Floor

Plan:
HPK1500119

Style:
FARMHOUSE

First Floor:
1,297 SQ. FT.

Second Floor:
1,390 SQ. FT.

Total:
2,687 SQ. FT.

Bonus Space:
229 SQ. FT.

Bedrooms:
3

Bathrooms:
2 1/2

Width:
60' - 0"

Depth:
44' - 0"

Foundation:
FINISHED WALKOUT BASEMENT

Plan:
HPK1500120

Style:
COUNTRY

First Floor:
880 SQ. FT.

Second Floor:
880 SQ. FT.

Total:
1,760 SQ. FT.

Bonus Space:
256 SQ. FT.

Bedrooms:
3

Bathrooms:
2 1/2

Width:
42' - 0"

Depth:
40' - 0"

Foundation:
UNFINISHED BASEMENT

First Floor

Second Floor

Plan:
HPK1500121

Style:
TRADITIONAL

First Floor:
805 SQ. FT.

Second Floor:
758 SQ. FT.

Total:
1,563 SQ. FT.

Bedrooms:
3

Bathrooms:
2 1/2

Width:
49' - 0"

Depth:
37' - 8"

Foundation:
CRAWLSPACE

Perfect for narrow lots, this practical, smaller home is a builder's dream. Ideal for a first home, it offers an open layout that adds a feeling of spaciousness. A fireplace on the first floor warms the family room, breakfast area, and kitchen. Upstairs houses the master suite, two family bedrooms, and a full bath. The laundry room is conveniently located on the second floor with the bedrooms.

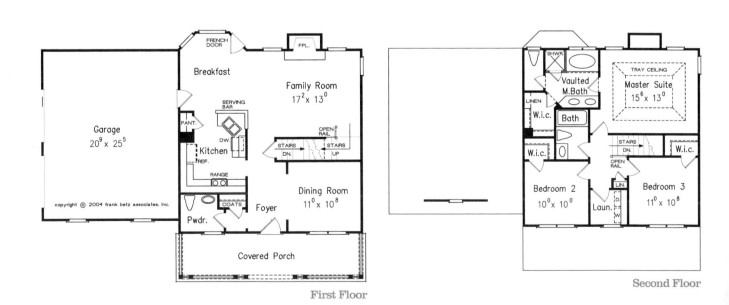

First Floor

Second Floor

First Floor

Second Floor

Plan:
HPK1500122

Style:
COUNTRY

First Floor:
1,040 SQ. FT.

Second Floor:
1,040 SQ. FT.

Total:
2,080 SQ. FT.

Bedrooms:
3

Bathrooms:
2 ½

Width:
48' - 0"

Depth:
38' - 2"

Foundation:
UNFINISHED
WALKOUT
BASEMENT

Plan:
HPK1500123

Style:	Bonus Space:	Width:
RANCH	**355 SQ. FT.**	**64' - 4"**
Square Footage:	Bedrooms:	Depth:
1,677	**3**	**49' - 10"**
	Bathrooms:	
	2	

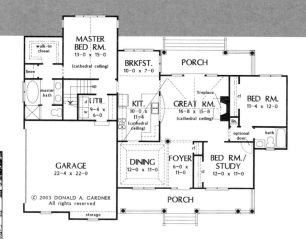

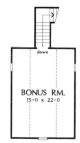

Plan:
HPK1500124

Style:
COUNTRY COTTAGE

First Floor:
1,524 SQ. FT.

Second Floor:
1,275 SQ. FT.

Total:
2,799 SQ. FT.

Bedrooms:
4

Bathrooms:
2 1/2

Width:
63' - 0"

Depth:
42' - 2"

Foundation:
UNFINISHED BASEMENT

Brick and siding accent the covered porch and wood trim adds color and dimension to the exterior of this two-story home. Standard nine-foot ceilings throughout the first floor and amenities such as a gas fireplace, furniture alcoves, a study with built-ins, angled stairs with wood rails, and a large work area in both the kitchen and laundry area make this a wonderful home for your family. A second-floor master bedroom enjoys a sloped ceiling and a bath with whirlpool tub, double-bowl vanity, and shower enclosure. The second-floor balcony overlooks the staircase and leads to three additional bedrooms.

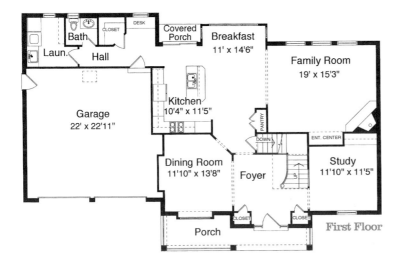

First Floor

Second Floor

DORMER

FUTURE
BONUS ROOM
21X11⁶

DN.
STAIRS

Optional Layout

Plan:
HPK1500125

Style:
TRADITIONAL

Square Footage:
2,714

Bonus Space:
378 SQ. FT.

Bedrooms:
3

Bathrooms:
2 ¹/₂

Width:
86' - 4"

Depth:
52' - 7"

Foundation:
**SLAB,
CRAWLSPACE**

Plan:
HPK1500126

Style:
COUNTRY COTTAGE

Square Footage:
2,050

Bonus Space:
418 SQ. FT.

Bedrooms:
4

Bathrooms:
3

Width:
60' - 0"

Depth:
56' - 0"

Foundation:
**CRAWLSPACE,
UNFINISHED
WALKOUT
BASEMENT, SLAB**

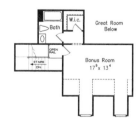

Plan:
HPK1500127

Style:
COUNTRY COTTAGE

First Floor:
1,921 SQ. FT.

Second Floor:
921 SQ. FT.

Total:
2,842 SQ. FT.

Bonus Space:
454 SQ. FT.

Bedrooms:
4

Bathrooms:
3 1/2

Width:
62' - 2"

Depth:
71' - 0"

Foundation:
CRAWLSPACE, UNFINISHED BASEMENT

© William E. Poole Designs, Inc.

A porch wraps around two sides and joins a screened porch in the rear, giving this country-style plan a true down-home appeal. The great room, which soars two stories high, enjoys a fireplace and two entries to the screened porch. It also opens easily into the breakfast alcove and is conveniently tied to the kitchen by an angled counter. A formal dining room is just to the right of the foyer. The luxurious master suite pampers with a walk-in closet, twin-sink vanity, garden tub, and step-up shower. Upstairs, three bedrooms share two baths and a loft study. Ample room is available to add a recreation room. A side-loading garage offers lots of room for storage.

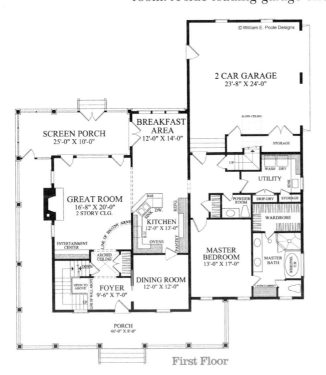

First Floor

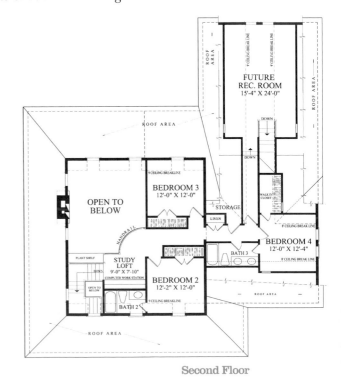

Second Floor

Plan:
HPK1500128

Style:
FARMHOUSE

First Floor:
3,438 SQ. FT.

Second Floor:
1,645 SQ. FT.

Total:
5,083 SQ. FT.

Bedrooms:
5

Bathrooms:
5

Width:
87' - 0"

Depth:
80' - 0"

Foundation:
UNFINISHED WALKOUT BASEMENT

Grand elegance brings out the Southern style of this farmhouse plan. The exterior is wrapped in a large sitting porch accented with columns and open pediments. Inside, a high-style staircase sits in the center of the formal foyer. To either side of the entry are a library with cozy fireplace and the spacious dining hall. To the rear of the layout, find the grand salon awash in natural light from the bank of windows gently bowed across the back wall. To the right, gorgeous family spaces include the keeping room with fireplace, morning room with veranda access, and the gourmet kitchen featuring two work islands and laundry studio. A secluded, first-floor master suite is filled with amenities designed for comfort; generous sitting area with firepalce, an oversized walk-in closet, His and Hers vanities, compartmentalized commode, soaking tub, and enclosed shower. The second floor provides for four comfortable family suites.

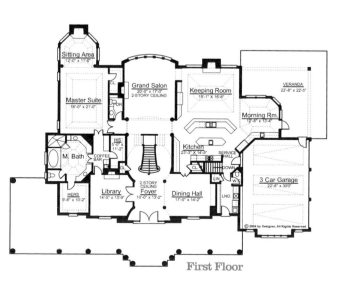

First Floor

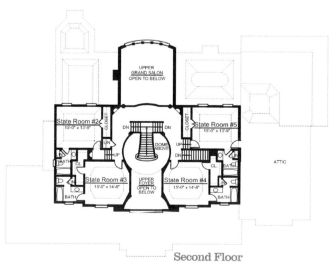

Second Floor

Farmhouses & Ranches

Plan:
HPK1500129

Style:
COUNTRY

First Floor:
1,848 SQ. FT.

Second Floor:
799 SQ. FT.

Total:
2,647 SQ. FT.

Bonus Space:
457 SQ. FT.

Bedrooms:
3

Bathrooms:
3 ¹/₂

Width:
81' - 0"

Depth:
49' - 8"

© 2003 Donald A. Gardner, Inc.

Circle-head transoms and decorative brackets soften strong angled gables, and bold columns define a welcoming country porch. Service entries from the garage, deck, and utility/mud room create convenience. Inside, a curved balcony separates the two-story foyer and great room, which is marked by columns at the entrance and warmed by a fireplace. A bay window extends the breakfast nook which is adjacent to the kitchen with an island. The first-floor master suite is well appointed, and the master bath is complete with dual-sink vanity, separate tub and shower, and nearby walk-in closets. Both second-floor bedrooms have their own private baths. This home is equipped with a bonus room, and outdoor living space is abundant.

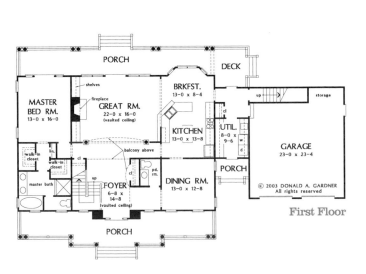

First Floor

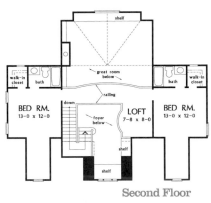

Second Floor

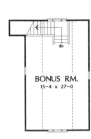

Farmhouses & Ranches

325 New Home Plans

Plan:
HPK1500130

Style:
COUNTRY COTTAGE

Square Footage:
2,539

Bonus Space:
636 SQ. FT.

Bedrooms:
4

Bathrooms:
2

Width:
98' - 0"

Depth:
53' - 11"

Foundation:
SLAB, UNFINISHED BASEMENT, CRAWLSPACE

Fine details from Stick Victorian and Second Empire styles create a strong country character. A wrapping porch surrounds the formal dining room and study. A large gallery guides traffic to three distinct living spaces. The private family quarters includes two secondary bedrooms with walk-in closets and a nearby full bath. The master suite displays comforts in the full bath, large closet, and private covered porch. Entertaining space includes the central great room with fireplace and more spaces to the front of the plan. Casual dining and food preparation is given an extra boost with a country kitchen and adjoining breakfast room. A loft and bonus space are perfect for later expansion.

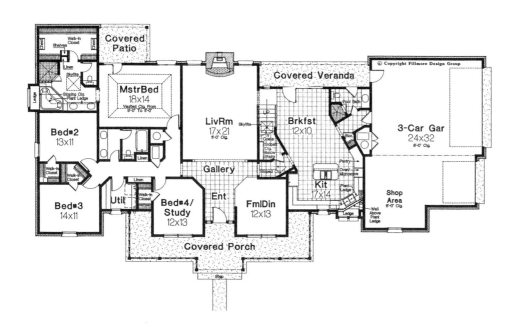

Plan:
HPK1500131

Style:
FARMHOUSE

First Floor:
1,778 SQ. FT.

Second Floor:
498 SQ. FT.

Total:
2,276 SQ. FT.

Bonus Space:
315 SQ. FT.

Bedrooms:
4

Bathrooms:
3

Width:
54' - 8"

Depth:
53' - 2"

First Floor

Second Floor

First Floor

Plan:
HPK1500132

Style:
FARMHOUSE

First Floor:
860 SQ. FT.

Second Floor:
840 SQ. FT.

Total:
1,700 SQ. FT.

Bedrooms:
3

Bathrooms:
1 1/2

Width:
30' - 0"

Depth:
29' - 0"

Foundation:
UNFINISHED BASEMENT

Second Floor

Plan:
HPK1500133

Style:
COUNTRY COTTAGE

First Floor:
2,070 SQ. FT.

Second Floor:
869 SQ. FT.

Total:
2,939 SQ. FT.

Bedrooms:
4

Bathrooms:
3 1/2

Width:
64' - 0"

Depth:
55' - 4"

Foundation:
CRAWLSPACE

This design incorporates all you could ask for and more into just under 3,000 square feet of space. The stone and siding on the exterior of this European home is both beautiful and welcoming. Enter into either the dining room or foyer from the covered front porch. Vaulted ceilings in the family room, keeping room, and first-floor master bath add to the elegance of the home. To the left, the kitchen easily serves the breakfast nook with convenient access to a back patio, or the keeping room via a serving bar. Three family bedrooms and two full baths are found on the second level.

First Floor

Second Floor

Plan:
HPK1500134

Style:
PRAIRIE

Square Footage:
1,880

Bonus Space:
346 SQ. FT.

Bedrooms:
3

Bathrooms:
2

Width:
68' - 6"

Depth:
49' - 0"

Foundation:
CRAWLSPACE, SLAB

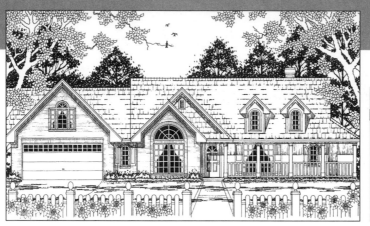

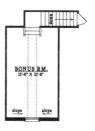

Plan:
HPK1500135

Style:
COUNTRY COTTAGE

Square Footage:
1,476

Bedrooms:
3

Bathrooms:
2

Width:
50' - 0"

Depth:
56' - 6"

Foundation:
CRAWLSPACE, SLAB

Plan:
HPK1500136

Style:
COUNTRY COTTAGE

First Floor:
1,866 SQ. FT.

Second Floor:
1,222 SQ. FT.

Total:
3,088 SQ. FT.

Bedrooms:
4

Bathrooms:
3 1/2

Width:
62' - 4"

Depth:
51' - 6"

Foundation:
CRAWLSPACE, UNFINISHED WALKOUT BASEMENT, SLAB

Triple dormers, a columned porch, and nested gables add interest to the exterior of this cottage home. An open, spacious interior provides space to entertain and areas for privacy. A large dining room sits just off of the vaulted foyer and within steps of the kitchen. Just beyond the entry, the family room features a lovely fireplace flanked by radius transom windows. A bayed breakfast area flows easily from the kitchen to the keeping room. The first-floor master suite offers a sitting bay perfect for reading, a vaulted bath, and oversized walk-in closet. Upstairs, three family suites each sport walk-in closets and share access to the entertainment room.

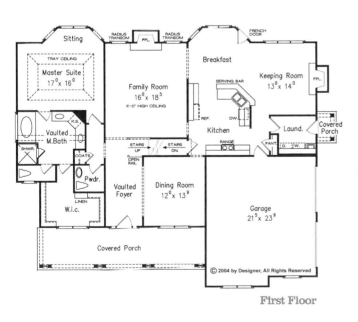

First Floor

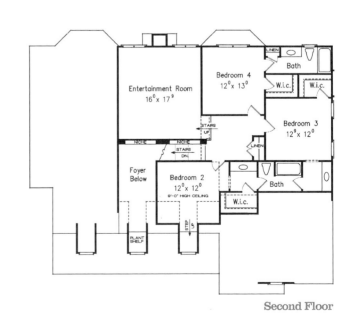

Second Floor

325 New Home Plans

Plan:
HPK1500137

Style:
COUNTRY COTTAGE

Square Footage:
2,018

Bedrooms:
4

Bathrooms:
2

Width:
64' - 10"

Depth:
56' - 2"

Foundation:
CRAWLSPACE, SLAB

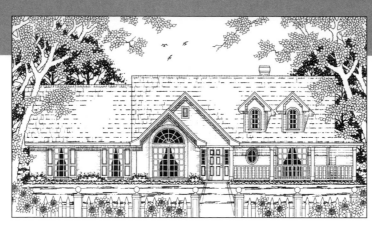

Plan:
HPK1500138

Style:
COUNTRY COTTAGE

Square Footage:
2,040

Bedrooms:
3

Bathrooms:
2

Width:
70' - 0"

Depth:
49' - 6"

Foundation:
CRAWLSPACE, SLAB

Plan:
HPK1500139

Style:
COUNTRY COTTAGE

Square Footage:
2,656

Bonus Space:
484 SQ. FT.

Bedrooms:
3

Bathrooms:
2 1/2

Width:
63' - 0"

Depth:
76' - 6"

Foundation:
CRAWLSPACE, UNFINISHED WALKOUT BASEMENT

An ideal mid-size home, this design makes great use of its space. The roomy master suite is enhanced by a tray ceiling, sitting area, and a private entrance to a covered porch. The family room boasts a vaulted ceiling, built-in cabinets, and a fireplace. The kitchen, with serving bar, conveniently serves the adjoining breakfast area and family room. Two additional family bedrooms share a full bath with a dual-sink vanity. Upstairs houses a bonus room with a walk-in closet and full bath, serving as a possible guest suite.

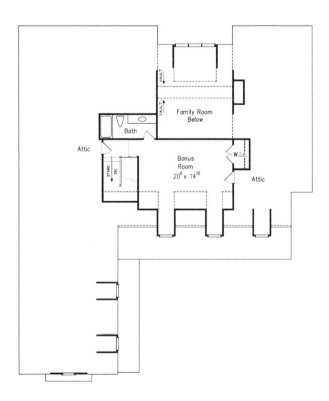

Plan:
HPK1500140

Style:
FARMHOUSE

First Floor:
1,809 SQ. FT.

Second Floor:
777 SQ. FT.

Total:
2,586 SQ. FT.

Bonus Space:
264 SQ. FT.

Bedrooms:
4

Bathrooms:
3 1/2

Width:
70' - 7"

Depth:
48' - 4"

Wrapping a traditional brick exterior with two country porches creates a modern exterior that's big on Southern charm. Bold columns and a metal roof welcome guests inside to an equally impressive interior. Both the foyer and family room have two-story ceilings. The family room includes such amenities as a fireplace, built-in shelves, and access to the rear porch. A bay window expands the breakfast nook, located adjacent to the U-shaped kitchen. The living room/study and bonus room add flexibility for changing needs. The master suite, conveniently located on the first level, is complete with linen shelves, two walk-in closets, and master bath featuring a double vanity, garden tub, separate shower, and private privy. The second level holds three more bedrooms, two bathrooms, bonus space, and an overlook to the beautiful family room.

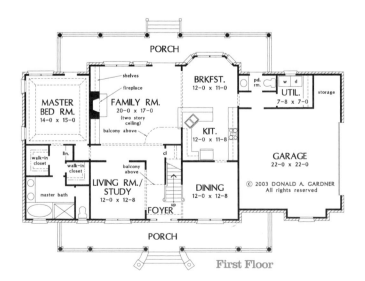

First Floor

Second Floor

Plan:
HPK1500141

Style:
COUNTRY COTTAGE

First Floor:
2,298 SQ. FT.

Second Floor:
1,039 SQ. FT.

Total:
3,337 SQ. FT.

Bedrooms:
4

Bathrooms:
3 1/2

Width:
65' - 0"

Depth:
56' - 10"

Foundation:
CRAWLSPACE

Charming on the outside and amenity-filled on the inside, this country cottage is sure to please. Front and rear covered porches offer outdoor living space. Inside, the dining room is defined by decorative columns and enhanced by a tray ceiling. The island kitchen flows easily with the keeping room and breakfast area while boasting ample counter space, a butler's pantry, and a convenient serving bar. A fireplace in the family room warms the space. The rear porch is accessed through French doors off the breakfast area. The adjoining family room, adorned with a coffered ceiling, features a second fireplace and built-in cabinets. A short hallway leads to the expansive master suite, enhanced by a tray ceiling, a sitting area, a huge walk-in closet, dual-sink vanities, a separate shower and tub, and a private toilet. The second floor houses three additional bedrooms sharing two full baths.

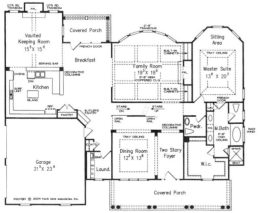

First Floor

Second Floor

Plan:
HPK1500142

Style:
COUNTRY COTTAGE

Square Footage:
2,487

Bonus Space:
306 SQ. FT.

Bedrooms:
3

Bathrooms:
2 ¹/2

Width:
61' - 6"

Depth:
67' - 6"

Foundation:
UNFINISHED WALKOUT BASEMENT, CRAWLSPACE

Optional Layout

Plan:
HPK1500143

Style:
COUNTRY COTTAGE

Square Footage:
2,057

Bonus Space:
327 SQ. FT.

Bedrooms:
3

Bathrooms:
2

Width:
56' - 4"

Depth:
62' - 0"

Foundation:
CRAWLSPACE, UNFINISHED WALKOUT BASEMENT, SLAB

Optional Layout

Farmhouses & Ranches

Plan:
HPK1500144

Style:
COUNTRY COTTAGE

First Floor:
2,224 SQ. FT.

Second Floor:
1,030 SQ. FT.

Total:
3,254 SQ. FT.

Bedrooms:
4

Bathrooms:
3

Width: 6
65' - 4"

Depth:
53' - 8"

Foundation:
CRAWLSPACE, UNFINISHED WALKOUT BASEMENT

Charming gables with Victorian-inspired trusses and a combination of exterior materials bring European Country flavor to the design. The interior features a thoughtful layout anchored by a large family room and breakfast nook at the center of the plan. Privacy spaces are at the right of the plan: a grand master suite including a sitting area and gorgeous bath, and a guest room of generous proportions. Upstairs reside the remaining two bedrooms and a shared bath, as well as a common area.

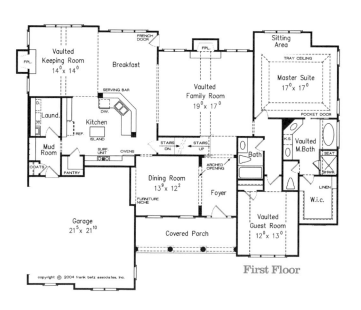

First Floor

Second Floor

Plan:
HPK1500145

Style:
COUNTRY COTTAGE

First Floor:
2,182 SQ. FT.

Second Floor:
980 SQ. FT.

Total:
3,162 SQ. FT.

Bedrooms:
4

Bathrooms:
3 1/2

Width:
70' - 4"

Depth:
65' - 0"

Foundation:
CRAWLSPACE, UNFINISHED WALKOUT BASEMENT, SLAB

Subtle Victorian details add charm to this spacious cottage home. A full-length covered porch is topped by twin dormers and an open-face gable. The entry opens to the dining room on the right and a vaulted family room to the back. A fireplace is the focal point of the family room. The breakfast nook adjoins the hardworking island kitchen and vaulted keeping room. The master suite enjoys privacy and all the amenities such as His and Hers walk-in closets and a tray ceiling. The second floor provides three family bedrooms, two full baths, and a computer alcove.

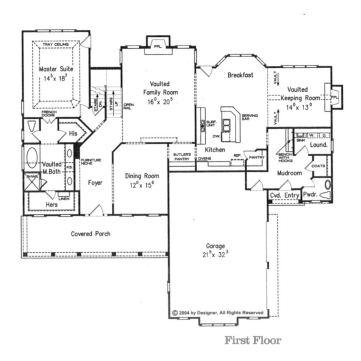

First Floor

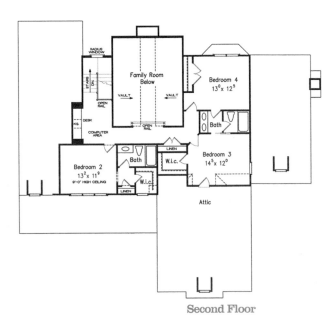

Second Floor

Plan:
HPK1500146

Style:
COUNTRY COTTAGE

First Floor:
1,725 SQ. FT.

Second Floor:
992 SQ. FT.

Total:
2,717 SQ. FT.

Bonus Space:
351 SQ. FT.

Bedrooms:
3

Bathrooms:
2 ¹/₂

Width:
46' - 0"

Depth:
85' - 0"

Foundation:
SLAB, CRAWLSPACE

A covered front porch provides three means of entrance—the front door into the foyer, a side door near the pantry, or French doors into the dining room. The island kitchen offers a serving bar to the coffer-ceilinged, hearth-warmed family room and access to the breakfast area, with yet another door leading outside. The master suite envelops the left side of the plan. The bath, with two sinks, compartmented toilet, and a separate tub and shower, is to be admired. Two bedrooms upstairs are convenienced by a spacious recreation room—so let the kids play!

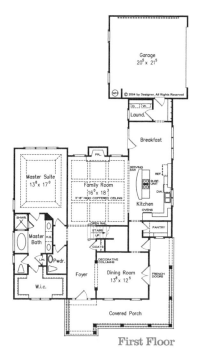

First Floor

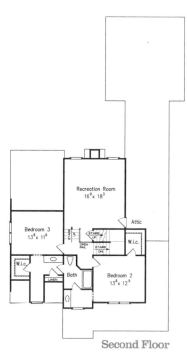

Second Floor

Plan:
HPK1500147

Style:
COUNTRY COTTAGE

Square Footage:
1,390

Bedrooms:
3

Bathrooms:
2

Width:
50' - 0"

Depth:
55' - 8"

Foundation:
UNFINISHED WALKOUT BASEMENT

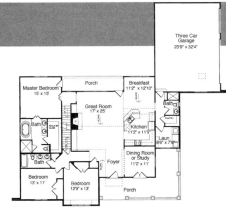

Plan:
HPK1500148

Style:
FARMHOUSE

Square Footage:
2,183

Bonus Space:
241 SQ. FT.

Bedrooms:
3

Bathrooms:
3

Width:
80' - 0"

Depth:
74' - 0"

Foundation:
UNFINISHED BASEMENT

Plan:
HPK1500149

Style:
COUNTRY COTTAGE

First Floor:
1,367 SQ. FT.

Second Floor:
1,492 SQ. FT.

Total:
2,859 SQ. FT.

Bedrooms:
4

Bathrooms:
2 1/2

Width:
58' - 0"

Depth:
45' - 0"

Foundation:
CRAWLSPACE, UNFINISHED WALKOUT BASEMENT

A two-story country cottage with a bevy of amenities, this home is sure to please. The two-story foyer is flanked by the formal living room and dining room, and leads into the spacious family room. A fireplace in the family room adds warmth to the space. A serving bar in the kitchen allows for casual meals and easy interaction between the breakfast area and family room. The master suite and three additional bedrooms are housed upstairs. The master suite, enhanced by a tray ceiling, boasts a private sitting room with window seat, a huge walk-in closet, a roomy bath with dual-sink vanities, a separate shower and tub, and a private toilet.

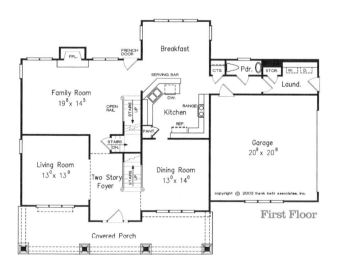

First Floor

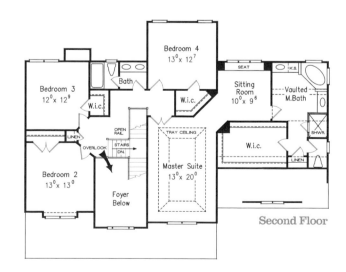

Second Floor

Plan:
HPK1500150

Style:
CRAFTSMAN

First Floor:
2,766 SQ. FT.

Second Floor:
881 SQ. FT.

Total:
3,647 SQ. FT.

Bonus Space:
407 SQ. FT.

Bedrooms:
3

Bathrooms:
3 1/2

Width:
92' - 5"

Depth:
71' - 10"

Using materials that combine the rugged frontier with stately elegance, this home has a grand, majestic facade. Four towering columns frame the dramatic barrel-vault entrance, and clerestories mimic the arched theme. Cedar shake, stone, and siding complement a metal roof over the front porch. The two-story foyer has impressive views of the study, dining room, living room, and balcony. Cathedral ceilings top the family room and master bedroom, and a vaulted ceiling tops the living room. Built-ins, three fireplaces, and a walk-in pantry add special touches. The master suite on the first floor and two family bedrooms upstairs boast private baths and walk-in closets. A library and flexible bonus space round out the second level.

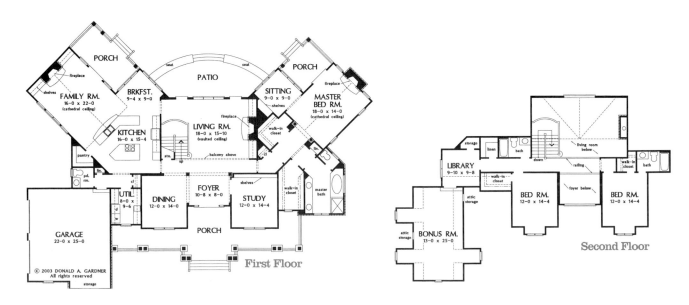

First Floor

Second Floor

Style:
COUNTRY COTTAGE

First Floor:
1,790 SQ. FT.

Second Floor:
797 SQ. FT.

Total:
2,587 SQ. FT.

Bedrooms:
4

Bathrooms:
3 1/2

Width:
64' - 4"

Depth:
50' - 0"

Foundation:
UNFINISHED BASEMENT

A brick and stone finish with arched windows, covered porch, and shingle siding trim decorate the exterior of this exciting home. The foyer showcases the angled staircase and opens generously to the great room. High windows above the French doors in the great room combine with the many other features to create a wonderful view as you enter the home. The spacious kitchen serves the breakfast room and dining room with equal ease and enjoys a bar with a seating, a window above the sink, and a walk-in pantry. The master bedroom suite boasts a sitting area with higher ceiling and deluxe dressing area. The whirlpool tub, double bowl vanity, and walk-in closet offer a luxurious retreat for the homeowner. Three second-floor bedrooms, one with a private bath, expand this home to serve the larger family or one that enjoys having overnight guests.

First Floor

Second Floor

Plan:
HPK1500317

Style:
EUROPEAN COTTAGE

First Floor:
2,351 SQ. FT.

Second Floor:
501 SQ. FT.

Total:
2,852 SQ. FT.

Bedrooms:
3

Bathrooms:
3

Width:
50' - 0"

Depth:
75' - 0"

Foundation:
SLAB, UNFINISHED BASEMENT

First Floor

Second Floor

Plan:
HPK1500318

Style:
EUROPEAN COTTAGE

Square Footage:
2,230

Bonus Space:
601 SQ. FT.

Bedrooms:
3

Bathrooms:
3

Width:
50' - 0"

Depth:
70' - 4"

Foundation:
SLAB, UNFINISHED BASEMENT

Plan:
HPK1500152

Style:
CRAFTSMAN

First Floor:
1,710 SQ. FT.

Second Floor:
774 SQ. FT.

Total:
2,484 SQ. FT.

Bedrooms:
4

Bathrooms:
3 ¹/₂

Width:
57' - 8"

Depth:
49' - 0"

Foundation:
UNFINISHED BASEMENT

This two-story home with stone, shake, and siding facade and a side-entry two-car garage presents spectacular curb appeal. Trim detail and a copper roof enhance the beauty of the exterior. A nine-foot first-floor ceiling height is standard throughout, with the great room and foyer ceilings soaring to a full two-story height. Columns and an arched opening frame the kitchen from the great room, and a boxed bay expands the breakfast area. A triple sliding glass door introduces an abundance of light and invites the activities to continue to the rear covered porch. A deluxe master bedroom suite boasts of a whirlpool tub, double bowl vanity, shower, and spacious walk-in closet. From the second-floor balcony a dramatic view is showcased to the great room and foyer. A secondary bedroom with a private bath makes a wonderful guest room.

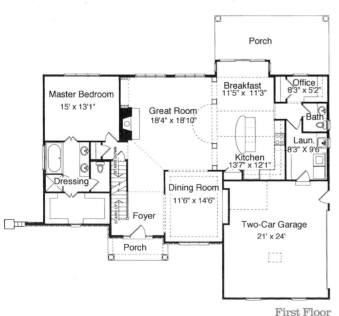

First Floor

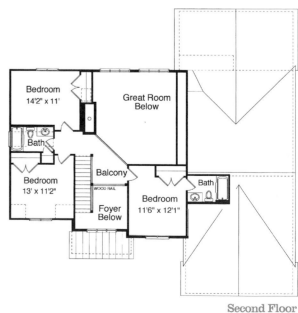

Second Floor

Plan:
HPK1500153

Style:
CONTEMPORARY

Square Footage:
2,160

Bedrooms:
4

Bathrooms:
3

Width:
61' - 8"

Depth:
52' - 0"

Foundation:
**SLAB,
UNFINISHED
BASEMENT**

Plan:
HPK1500154

Style:
TRADITIONAL

Square Footage:
2,420

Bonus Space:
372 SQ. FT.

Bedrooms:
3

Bathrooms:
2 ½

Width:
65' - 10"

Depth:
68' - 10"

Foundation:
**CRAWLSPACE,
SLAB,
UNFINISHED
BASEMENT**

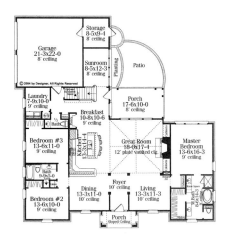

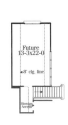

Plan:
HPK1500155

Style:
EUROPEAN COTTAGE

First Floor:
1,795 SQ. FT.

Second Floor:
591 SQ. FT.

Total:
2,386 SQ. FT.

Bonus Space:
298 SQ. FT.

Bedrooms:
3

Bathrooms:
2 ¹/₂

Width:
62' - 0"

Depth:
55' - 4"

Foundation:
UNFINISHED BASEMENT

An exterior that showcases multiple gables and a brick and stone facade creates a home that is equally decorative inside. The foyer introduces a beautiful great room wtih built-in cabinets, gas fireplace, 12-foot ceilings, and an arch-top window on the rear wall. The grand opening to the dining room expands the great room and multiple windows allow an abundance of light to warm the combined living areas. A nine-foot ceiling tops the dining room, adding variety and intimacy to entertaining. French doors at the rear are an invitation to the delightful screened porch. The spacious kitchen and breakfast area boast a work-top island, large pantry, and nine-foot ceilings that slope up at the breakfast area for a dramatic effect. The master bedroom suite enjoys a whirlpool tub, shower enclosure, and private commode room. Access to the laundry room from the master bath adds convenience to the homeowner. Split stairs lead to a second floor where a private computer area and two additional bedrooms complete this wonderful home. A bonus space above the garage allows for expansion of the living space as desired.

First Floor

Second Floor

Plan:
HPK1500156

Style:
TRADITIONAL

Square Footage:
1,847

Bedrooms:
3

Bathrooms:
2 ¹/₂

Width:
65' - 0"

Depth:
56' - 8"

Foundation:
CRAWLSPACE, SLAB, UNFINISHED BASEMENT

Plan:
HPK1500157

Style:
TRADITIONAL

Square Footage:
1,926

Bedrooms:
4

Bathrooms:
2

Width:
63' - 10"

Depth:
56' - 6"

Foundation:
CRAWLSPACE, SLAB, UNFINISHED BASEMENT

Urban Designs & Traditionals

325 New Home Plans

Plan:
HPK1500158

Style:
TRADITIONAL

First Floor:
935 SQ. FT.

Second Floor:
1,150 SQ. FT.

Total:
2,085 SQ. FT.

Bedrooms:
4

Bathrooms:
2 1/2

Width:
50' - 0"

Depth:
36' - 8"

Foundation:
UNFINISHED BASEMENT

This wonderful floor plan offers convenience and style to provide many years of enjoyment and comfort for the growing family. The foyer introduces a turned staircase with wood trim and a large great room with a corner fireplace and windows to the rear yard. The grand opening to the dining area and snack bar expands the gathering space for a roomy look and feel. The kitchen offers an abundance of counter space, cabinets, and a pantry for added storage. Entry from the garage through a hall creates an orderly and accessible traffic flow. The second-floor master suite showcases a raised ceiling and dressing area with whirlpool tub, double-bowl vanity, shower enclosure, and two walk-in closets. Three additional bedrooms complete this wonderfully designed home.

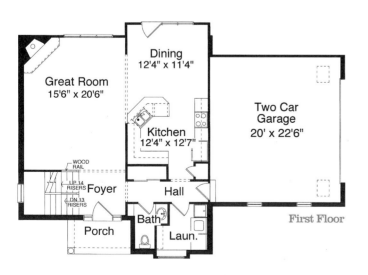

First Floor

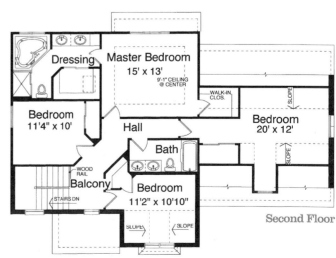

Second Floor

Plan:
HPK1500159

Style:
TRADITIONAL

First Floor:
854 SQ. FT.

Second Floor:
875 SQ. FT.

Total:
1,729 SQ. FT.

Bonus Space:
242 SQ. FT.

Bedrooms:
3

Bathrooms:
2 ¹/₂

Width:
45' - 10"

Depth:
37' - 5"

Foundation:
CRAWLSPACE

First Floor

Second Floor

First Floor

Plan:
HPK1500160

Style:	Total:	Width:
TRADITIONAL	**2,804 SQ. FT.**	**56' - 4"**
First Floor:	Bedrooms:	Depth:
1,723 SQ. FT.	**4**	**72' - 0"**
Second Floor:	Bathrooms:	Foundation:
1,081 SQ. FT.	**3 ¹/₂**	**CRAWLSPACE**

Second Floor

Plan:
HPK1500161

Style:
ADAM STYLE

First Floor:
1,933 SQ. FT.

Second Floor:
787 SQ. FT.

Total:
2,720 SQ. FT.

Bedrooms:
4

Bathrooms:
2 ¹/₂

Width:
56' - 0"

Depth:
48' - 0"

Foundation:
UNFINISHED WALKOUT BASEMENT

A modern, traditional-style home featuring all the comforts for a busy lifestyle. The first-floor master suite offers twin walk-in closets, a sumptuous bath with separate vanities, and shower enclosure. A private study sits just to the front of the home and can easily be converted into a home office. The dining room and two-story grand room are great spots for entertaining during the holidays or other occasions. The kitchen is outfitted with an island, adjoining keeping room, and double French doors to the rear deck. Upstairs, three family bedrooms share a full hall bath and a balcony alcove.

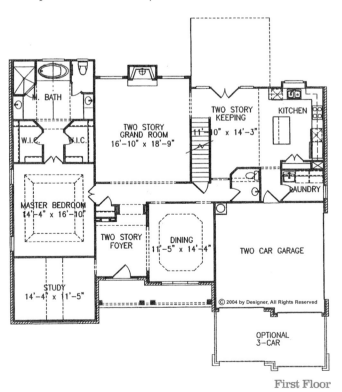

First Floor

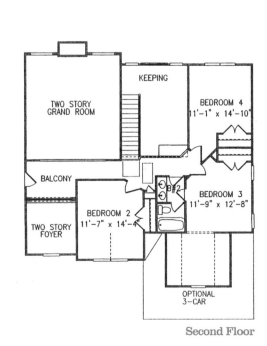

Second Floor

This home, as shown in photographs, may differ from the actual blueprints. For more detailed information, please check the floor plans carefully.

Plan:
HPK1500162

Style:
FRENCH

First Floor:
1,676 SQ. FT.

Second Floor:
1,408 SQ. FT.

Total:
3,084 SQ. FT.

Bedrooms:
4

Bathrooms:
2 1/2

Width:
61' - 6"

Depth:
44' - 6"

Foundation:
UNFINISHED WALKOUT BASEMENT

A solid brick exterior is adorned with brick quoins and limestone keys. Inside, nine-foot ceilings are typical throughout the first floor. Angled stairs decorate the foyer, and a dining room offers a dropped soffit at the perimeter creating a tray ceiling. The butler's pantry between the kitchen and dining room adds convenience. A gas fireplace and six-foot tall windows decorate the great room. The secluded library provides privacy for work-at-home projects. The master suite offers a sloped ceiling and a luxurious bath that includes a double-bowl vanity, linen cabinet, whirlpool tub, and a shower enclosure. Three additional bedrooms, each with a spacious walk-in closet, complete this family-friendly home.

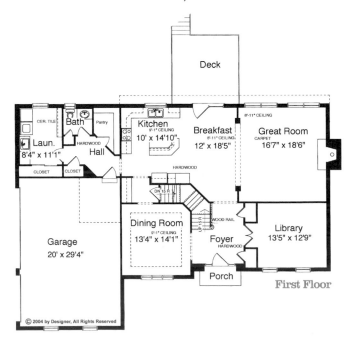

First Floor

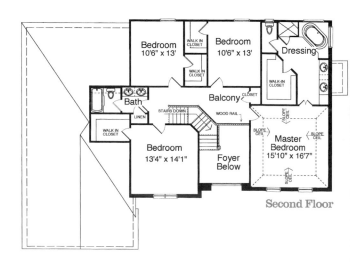

Second Floor

Plan:
HPK1500163

Style:
FRENCH

First Floor:
2,352 SQ. FT.

Second Floor:
952 SQ. FT.

Total:
3,304 SQ. FT.

Bedrooms:
5

Bathrooms:
4

Width:
61' - 0"

Depth:
66' - 8"

Foundation:
**SLAB,
UNFINISHED
WALKOUT
BASEMENT**

Five gables top this traditional home's exterior. A formal entry is flanked by a vaulted living room and by a dining room with tray ceiling. If you need a larger entertaining space, the two-sotry grand room fits the bill. A fireplace with built-ins provides the focal point and is enjoyed by the breakfast bay and the kitchen. A guest bedrooms sits just behind the kitchen. Fine appointments in the master suite create a luxurious place to destress. Four secondary bedrooms share two full baths and an entertainment loft with media built-ins. Unfinished bonus space can be used for storage.

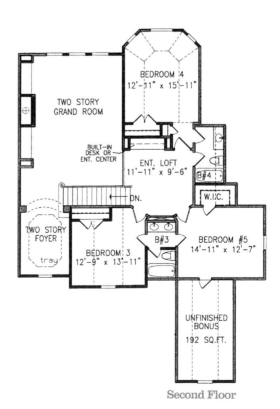

First Floor

Second Floor

© 2004 by Designer, All Rights Reserved

Plan:
HPK1500164

Style:
TRADITIONAL

First Floor:
2,469 SQ. FT.

Second Floor:
1,786 SQ. FT.

Total:
4,255 SQ. FT.

Bedrooms:
4

Bathrooms:
4

Width:
66' - 8"

Depth:
69' - 3"

Foundation:
CRAWLSPACE

A stately brick facade expresses its traditional style with corner quoins, an arched entry, and keystone-topped lintels. Inside, an open floor plan accentuates the ease and flow of one room to another. Decorative columns add definition to the dining room and a fireplace and built-ins give the gathering room some warmth and charm. Double French doors introduce the patio, a perfect spot for enjoying the weather. The master suite also enjoys patio access and is further pampered by a large walk-in closet, dual-sink vanity, soaking tub, and shower enclosure. A guest suite or den can be found near the kitchen. Three family bedrooms each sport walk-in closets and access to a second-floor recreation room and home office.

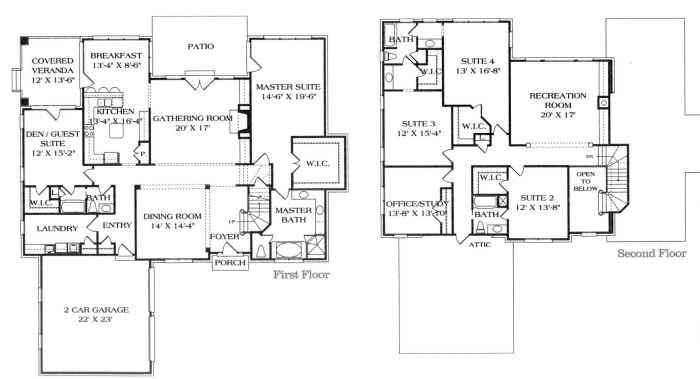

Urban Designs & Traditionals

325 New Home Plans

Plan:
HPK1500165

Style:
TRADITIONAL
First Floor:
2,193 SQ. FT.
Second Floor:
1,004 SQ. FT.
Total:
3,197 SQ. FT.
Bedrooms:
4
Bathrooms:
4 ½
Width:
67' - 0"
Depth:
74' - 4"
Foundation:
CRAWLSPACE

Dramatic, soaring entryway, steep rooflines, and elegant corner quoins add breathtaking depth and beauty to this home design. Formal spaces flank the foyer and more casual rooms sit to the rear. An open layout between the family room, breakfast bay, and kitchen inspires interaction. The master suite features a tray ceiling, terrace access, large walk-in closet, and full bath. Three secondary bedrooms enjoy private baths and walk-in closets. A spacious computer and media room will be a favorite gathering spot for family friends.

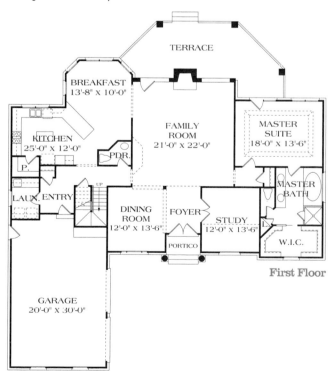

First Floor

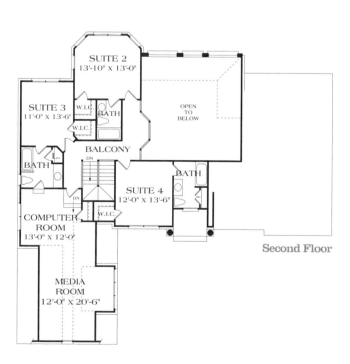

Second Floor

Plan:
HPK1500319

Style:
EUROPEAN COTTAGE

Square Footage:
2,221

Bonus Space:
602 SQ. FT.

Bedrooms:
3

Bathrooms:
3

Width:
50' - 0"

Depth:
70' - 4"

Foundation:
SLAB, UNFINISHED BASEMENT

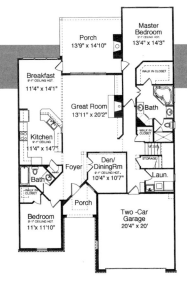

Plan:
HPK1500320

Style:
EUROPEAN COTTAGE

Square Footage:
1,820

Bonus Space:
592 SQ. FT.

Bedrooms:
3

Bathrooms:
3

Width:
42' - 0"

Depth:
70' - 8"

Foundation:
SLAB, UNFINISHED BASEMENT

Plan:

HPK1500321

Style:
EUROPEAN COTTAGE

Square Footage:
1,832

Bonus Space:
651 SQ. FT.

Bedrooms:
3

Bathrooms:
3

Width:
42' - 0"

Depth:
75' - 0"

Foundation:
SLAB, UNFINISHED BASEMENT

Plan:

HPK1500166

Style:	Total:	Width:
TUDOR	**2,353 SQ. FT.**	**45' - 0"**
Main Level:	Bedrooms:	Depth:
1,586 SQ. FT.	**5**	**49' - 9"**
Lower Level:	Bathrooms:	Foundation:
767 SQ. FT.	**3**	**UNFINISHED BASEMENT**

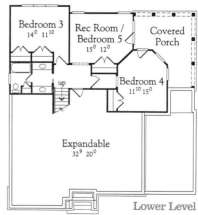

Plan:
HPK1500167

Style:
TRADITIONAL

First Floor:
1,498 SQ. FT.

Second Floor:
1,275 SQ. FT.

Total:
2,773 SQ. FT.

Bedrooms:
4

Bathrooms:
2 1/2

Width:
63' - 0"

Depth:
41' - 2"

Foundation:
UNFINISHED BASEMENT

First Floor

Second Floor

Plan:
HPK1500168

Style:
TRADITIONAL

First Floor:
1,522 SQ. FT.

Second Floor:
1,305 SQ. FT.

Total:
2,827 SQ. FT.

Bedrooms:
4

Bathrooms:
2 1/2

Width:
63' - 0"

Depth:
41' - 2"

Foundation:
UNFINISHED BASEMENT

First Floor

Second Floor

First Floor

Second Floor

This home, as shown in photographs, may differ from the actual blueprints. For more detailed information, please check the floor plans carefully.

Plan:
HPK1500169

Style:
COLONIAL

First Floor:
1,056 SQ. FT.

Second Floor:
967 SQ. FT.

Total:
2,023 SQ. FT.

Bonus Space:
291 SQ. FT.

Bedrooms:
3

Bathrooms:
2 1/2

Width:
45' - 0"

Depth:
40' - 0"

Foundation:
CRAWLSPACE

Plan:
HPK1500322

Style:	Total:	Bathrooms:
TRADITIONAL	**2,171 SQ. FT.**	**2 1/2**
First Floor:	Bonus Space:	Width:
1,639 SQ. FT.	**335 SQ. FT.**	**49' - 0"**
Second Floor:	Bedrooms:	Depth:
532 SQ. FT.	**3**	**60' - 0"**

First Floor

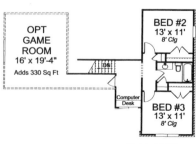

Second Floor

Plan:
HPK1500170

Style:
TRADITIONAL

Square Footage:
1,915

Bedrooms:
3

Bathrooms:
2

Width:
45' - 10"

Depth:
62' - 6"

Foundation:
CRAWLSPACE

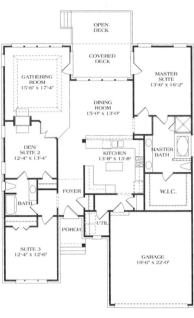

Plan:
HPK1500171

Style:
COUNTRY COTTAGE

Square Footage:
1,895

Bedrooms:
3

Bathrooms:
2

Width:
66' - 0"

Depth:
69' - 0"

Foundation:
UNFINISHED BASEMENT

Plan:
HPK1500172

Style:
COUNTRY COTTAGE

Square Footage:
1,833

Bedrooms:
3

Bathrooms:
2

Width:
68' - 0"

Depth:
49' - 5"

Foundation:
CRAWLSPACE, SLAB, UNFINISHED BASEMENT

Optional Layout

Plan:
HPK1500173

Style:	Bathrooms:	Foundation:
TRADITIONAL	**2**	**CRAWLSPACE, SLAB, UNFINISHED BASEMENT**
Square Footage:	Width:	
2,339	**72' - 8"**	
Bedrooms:	Depth:	
3	**61' - 4"**	

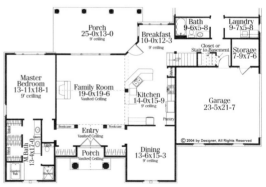

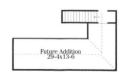

Plan:
HPK1500174

Style:
TRADITIONAL

Square Footage:
1,204

Bedrooms:
3

Bathrooms:
2

Width:
43' - 1"

Depth:
47' - 1"

Foundation:
SLAB

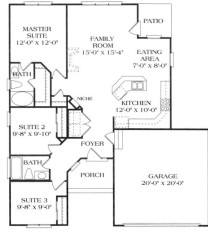

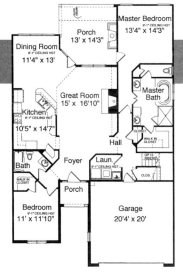

Plan:
HPK1500323

Style:
COUNTRY COTTAGE

Square Footage:
1,606

Bonus Space:
496 SQ. FT.

Bedrooms:
3

Bathrooms:
3

Width:
40' - 0"

Depth:
64' - 2"

Foundation:
SLAB, UNFINISHED BASEMENT

ORDER BLUEPRINTS 24 HOURS, 7 DAYS A WEEK, AT 1-800-521-6797 OR EPLANS.COM

Garage
21⁴ 21⁴

Bedrm. 2
12⁶ 12⁰

Master
Bedroom
15⁰ 16⁰

Study/
Guest
10⁰ 13⁰

Kit.
11⁰ 12⁰

Dining
12² 15⁴

Living
17⁶ 15⁴

Porch

Plan:
HPK1500175

Style:
TRADITIONAL

Square Footage:
1,875

Bedrooms:
2

Bathrooms:
2

Width:
31' - 0"

Depth:
81' - 2"

Foundation:
SLAB

Plan:
HPK1500176

Style:
COUNTRY COTTAGE

Square Footage:
1,550

Bedrooms:
3

Bathrooms:
2

Width:
50' - 0"

Depth:
55' - 0"

Foundation:
SLAB

Covered Patio
38⁸ · 9⁴

Master Bedroom
15⁰ · 12⁸

Nook

Family Room
16⁴ · 17⁸

Bedroom 2
11⁰ · 11⁰

w.i.c.

pan.

Bath 2

Mstr. Bath

Kitchen
11⁴ · 9⁴

Laundry

Foyer

Bedroom 3
12⁴ · 12⁰

2 Car Garage
19⁴ · 19⁰

Dining Rm.
10⁸ · 11⁰

Entry

Plan:
HPK1500177

Style:
ADAM STYLE

First Floor:
1,792 SQ. FT.

Second Floor:
899 SQ. FT.

Total:
2,691 SQ. FT.

Bedrooms:
4

Bathrooms:
2 1/2

Width:
32' - 9"

Depth:
99' - 5"

Foundation:
SLAB

First Floor

Second Floor

Plan:
HPK1500178

Style:	Total:	Width:
ADAM STYLE	**2,478 SQ. FT.**	**29' - 2"**
First Floor:	Bedrooms:	Depth:
1,545 SQ. FT.	**4**	**81' - 2"**
Second Floor:	Bathrooms:	Foundation:
933 SQ. FT.	**2 1/2**	**SLAB**

First Floor

Second Floor

Plan:
HPK1500179

Style:
TRADITIONAL

First Floor:
1,260 SQ. FT.

Second Floor:
1,057 SQ. FT.

Total:
2,317 SQ. FT.

Bedrooms:
5

Bathrooms:
2 1/2

Width:
35' - 0"

Depth:
56' - 0"

Foundation:
SLAB

At home in the city, this narrow-lot design takes advantatge of street views. A rear-loading two-car garage is accessed by a rear porch and the breakfast room. The adjoining C-shaped kitchen is only steps from the formal dining room. A warming fireplace can be enjoyed in the great room and even the dining room. A first-floor master suite adds convenience and comfort to the homeowner. Two walk-in closets, dual-sink vanity, soaking tub, and enclosed shower pamper and disolve streess. The second floor is home four bedrooms—or three bedrooms and a loft. A roomy laundry space is located on the second floor.

First Floor

Second Floor

325
New Home Plans

Plan:
HPK1500180

Style:
TRADITIONAL

First Floor:
1,635 SQ. FT.

Second Floor:
917 SQ. FT.

Total:
2,552 SQ. FT.

Bonus Space:
271 SQ. FT.

Bedrooms:
3

Bathrooms:
2 1/2

Width:
46' - 10"

Depth:
61' - 2"

Foundation:
CRAWLSPACE

First Floor

Second Floor

Photo courtesy of Living Concepts.
This home as shown in photographs may differ from the actual blueprints

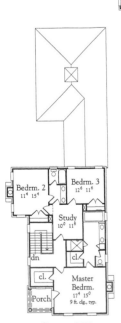

First Floor

Second Floor

Plan:
HPK1500181

Style:	**Total:**	**Width:**
ADAM STYLE	**2,778 SQ. FT.**	**21' - 8"**
First Floor:	**Bedrooms:**	**Depth:**
1,587 SQ. FT.	**3**	**93' - 8"**
Second Floor:	**Bathrooms:**	**Foundation:**
1,191 SQ. FT.	**2 1/2**	**SLAB**

First Floor

- Garage 21⁴ 21¹
- Screen Porch
- Kit. 11⁰ 15⁴
- Family 17⁵ 15⁴
- Dining 17⁴ 13¹¹
- up
- Foyer
- Living 17⁴ 15⁹
- Porch

Second Floor

- Bedrm 2 10¹¹ 16⁸
- Bedrm 3 11⁵ 12¹¹
- Master Bedroom 17⁴ 15⁹
- Balc.

Plan:
HPK1500182

Style:
TRADITIONAL

First Floor:
1,239 SQ. FT.

Second Floor:
1,087 SQ. FT.

Total:
2,326 SQ. FT.

Bedrooms:
3

Bathrooms:
2 ¹/₂

Width:
29' - 10"

Depth:
46' - 11"

Foundation:
SLAB

Plan:
HPK1500183

Style: **ADAM STYLE**	Total: **2,225 SQ. FT.**	Width: **36' - 2"**
First Floor: **1,369 SQ. FT.**	Bedrooms: **4**	Depth: **71' - 6"**
Second Floor: **856 SQ. FT.**	Bathrooms: **2 ¹/₂**	Foundation: **SLAB**

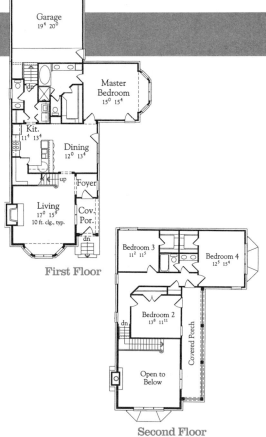

First Floor

- Garage 19⁴ 20⁰
- Master Bedroom 15⁰ 15⁴
- Kit. 11¹ 13⁴
- Dining 12⁰ 13⁴
- up
- Foyer
- Living 17⁰ 15⁹ 10 ft. clg., typ.
- Cov. Por.
- dn

Second Floor

- Bedroom 3 11² 11⁵
- Bedroom 4 12⁵ 15⁴
- Bedroom 2 13⁸ 11¹¹
- dn
- Covered Porch
- Open to Below

Plan:
HPK1500184

Style:
GEORGIAN

First Floor:
1,150 SQ. FT.

Second Floor:
1,194 SQ. FT.

Total:
2,344 SQ. FT.

Bedrooms:
4

Bathrooms:
3

Width:
38' - 4"

Depth:
64' - 1"

Foundation:
CRAWLSPACE

This eye-catching facade is dominated by Colonial elements, such as the double portico and classic pediment. The well-planned interior begins with an open arrangement of the living and dining rooms. The kitchen serves the breakfast room and dining area with ease. A study/guest room has use of a hall bath. Upstairs, two family bedrooms enjoy walk-in closets and share a bath. The master suite provides two walk-in closets and a private balcony.

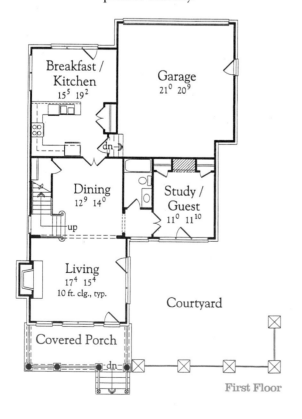

First Floor

Second Floor

ORDER BLUEPRINTS 24 HOURS, 7 DAYS A WEEK, AT 1-800-521-6797 OR EPLANS.COM

Plan:
HPK1500185

© William E. Poole Designs, Inc.

Style:
COLONIAL

First Floor:
1,625 SQ. FT.

Second Floor:
849 SQ. FT.

Total:
2,474 SQ. FT.

Bonus Space:
283 SQ. FT.

Bedrooms:
4

Bathrooms:
3 ½

Width:
50' - 2"

Depth:
71' - 1"

Foundation:
CRAWLSPACE

This four-bedroom Colonial home is designed with comfort and functionality in mind. Indoor and outdoor living combine with front and rear porches, which are accessible from the foyer and spacious great room. Serving meals is a breeze, whether using the dining room for a formal setting or sitting down for a casual meal in the breakfast nook, conveniently placed adjacent to the kitchen. Secluded in the back left corner of the home is the master suite, and adjoining master bath, situated for privacy. The second level holds three family bedrooms and two full baths—with the future rec room completing this floor, there is plenty of space for a growing family.

First Floor

Second Floor

Plan:
HPK1500324

Style:
**FRENCH
COUNTRY**

Square Footage:
2,640

Bedrooms:
3

Bathrooms:
2 1/2

Width:
50' - 0"

Depth:
70' - 4"

Escape to the French countryside in your private cottage. A hipped dormer anchoring a pitched roof announces this house of distinction. A rounded fanlight graces your entryway, upon which you are rewarded with a distant view of the gathering room down the main hallway. Upon touring the kitchen—complete with separate dining and eating areas—and bedrooms on the first floor, be sure not to miss the upstairs with exercise, game, and rec rooms, bar, and extra bedroom with attached bath, along with plentiful storage space.

Urban Designs & Traditionals

New Home Plans

Plan:
HPK1500186

Style:
FRENCH COUNTRY

First Floor:
2,074 SQ. FT.

Second Floor:
994 SQ. FT.

Total:
3,068 SQ. FT.

Bedrooms:
4

Bathrooms:
4 1/2

Width:
40' - 4"

Depth:
86' - 4"

Foundation:
SLAB

The stately look of this two-story townhouse is further enhanced with French-European style. A covered front porch welcomes you inside, where the living room warmed by a fireplace extends into the formal dining room. The kitchen offers an island/snack counter that serves the breakfast/family room, warmed by a second fireplace. The first-floor master suite is located to the front of the plan and includes a private bath and two walk-in closets. A garage and utility room complete the first floor. Three additional bedrooms reside upstairs—each has its own walk-in closet and private bath.

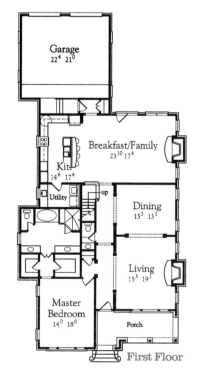

First Floor

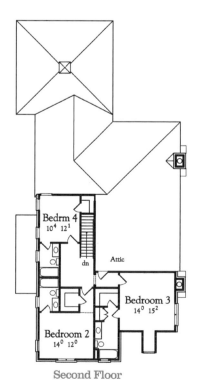

Second Floor

Plan:
HPK1500187

Style:
TRADITIONAL

First Floor:
1,235 SQ. FT.

Second Floor:
541 SQ. FT.

Total:
1,776 SQ. FT.

Bedrooms:
3

Bathrooms:
3

Width:
34' - 9"

Depth:
56' - 1"

Foundation:
SLAB

Arches, dormers, a bay window, and porch columns set off this lovely home. The varied vernacular of this stunning design promotes the eclectic nature of the neighborhood. Inside, the foyer directs guests to the formal dining room or to the rear of the plan to warm their hands by the hearth in the family room. The screened porch offers a summertime retreat and great indoor/outdoor flow. A master suite, thoughtfully placed just off the foyer, provides a bay window and a compartmented bath.

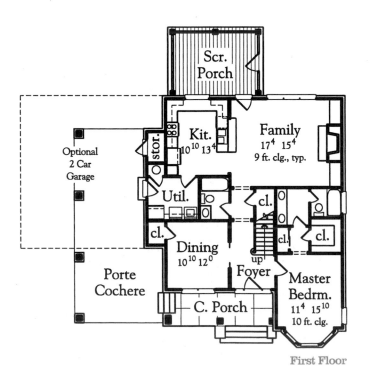

First Floor

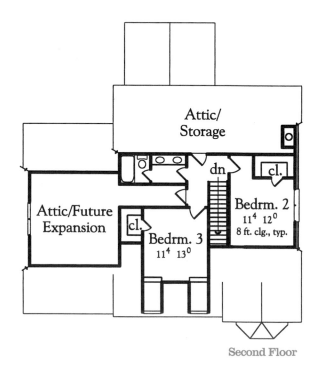

Second Floor

Urban Designs & Traditionals

325
New Home Plans

First Floor

Second Floor

Plan:
HPK1500188

Style:
TRADITIONAL

First Floor:
1,660 SQ. FT.

Second Floor:
943 SQ. FT.

Total:
2,603 SQ. FT.

Bedrooms:
3

Bathrooms:
3 1/2

Width:
30' - 10"

Depth:
102' - 10"

Foundation:
SLAB

Plan:
HPK1500189

Style: **TRADITIONAL**	Total: **1,776 SQ. FT.**	Depth: **36' - 0"**
First Floor: **865 SQ. FT.**	Bedrooms: **3**	Foundation: **SLAB, CRAWLSPACE, UNFINISHED BASEMENT**
Second Floor: **911 SQ. FT.**	Bathrooms: **2 1/2**	
	Width: **35' - 0"**	

First Floor

Second Floor

Plan:
HPK1500190

Style:
COLONIAL

First Floor:
1,379 SQ. FT.

Second Floor:
1,593 SQ. FT.

Total:
2,972 SQ. FT.

Bonus Space:
410 SQ. FT.

Bedrooms:
4

Bathrooms:
3

Width:
41' - 10"

Depth:
68' - 5"

Foundation:
SLAB

This stately facade displays enchanting elements, such as a piazza, an upper portico, and charming shutters. The entryway, set off the covered porch, leads one step down to the formal dining room or living room, which has a fireplace. The gourmet kitchen serves a convenient snack counter. A study/guest room and nearby hall bath complete this floor. The splendid master suite has its own hearth, a lavish bath, and private balcony. A staircase leads up to a loft area—a perfect space for a home office.

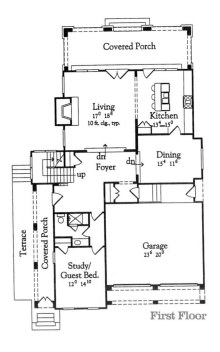

First Floor

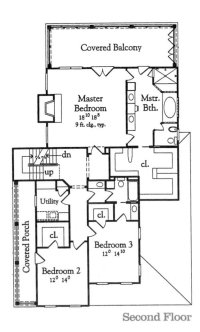

Second Floor

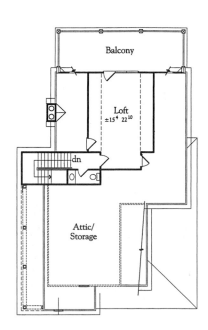

Plan:
HPK1500191

Style:
TRADITIONAL

First Floor:
1,344 SQ. FT.

Second Floor:
1,260 SQ. FT.

Total:
2,604 SQ. FT.

Bonus Space:
393 SQ. FT.

Bedrooms:
4

Bathrooms:
3

Width:
37' - 11"

Depth:
66' - 4"

Foundation:
SLAB

This unique stucco facade is gently flavored with Mediterranean elements, such as the arched decorative columns and hip standing-seam roof. A well-defined foyer announces the formal rooms, including a flex study or guest room, and a living room, which shares its through-fireplace with the casual living area. On the second floor, the master suite is positively spoiled by two walk-in closets and a sumptuous bath. Each of the secondary bedrooms has a walk-in closet.

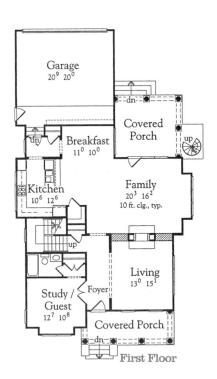

First Floor

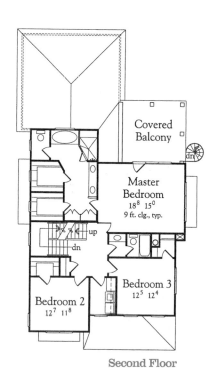

Second Floor

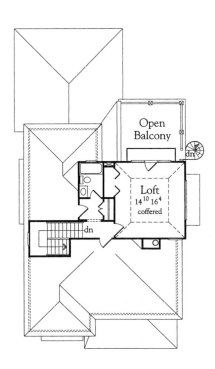

Plan:
HPK1500192

Style:
LAKEFRONT

First Floor:
1,290 SQ. FT.

Second Floor:
548 SQ. FT.

Total:
1,838 SQ. FT.

Bedrooms:
3

Bathrooms:
2 ¹/₂

Width:
38' - 0"

Depth:
51' - 0"

Foundation:
CRAWLSPACE, UNFINISHED BASEMENT

A delightful facade is made more attractive by a standing-seam roof. Highlighting the interior is the gourmet dream kitchen, featuring an island, eating bar, and bumped-out bay window. The great room gets a modern lift from the fireplace, French doors, and built-in entertainment center. An open dining room enjoys double French doors that lead to the covered porch. The master suite is tucked away for privacy and includes a full bath and walk-in closet. Upstairs, two bedrooms share a bath.

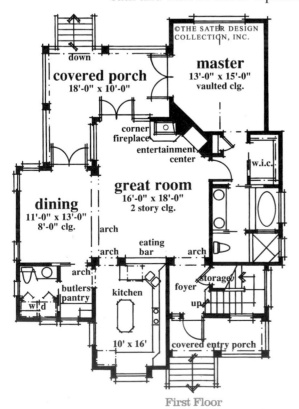

First Floor

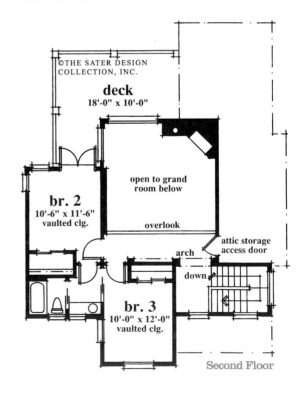

Second Floor

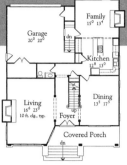

First Floor

Second Floor

Plan:
HPK1500193

Style:
GREEK REVIVAL

First Floor:
1,318 SQ. FT.

Second Floor:
1,810 SQ. FT.

Total:
3,128 SQ. FT.

Bonus Space:
250 SQ. FT.

Bedrooms:
3

Bathrooms:
3 1/2

Width:
39' - 8"

Depth:
51' - 9"

Foundation:
CRAWLSPACE

First Floor

Plan:
HPK1500194

Style: **COUNTRY COTTAGE**	Total: **2,684 SQ. FT.**	Width: **40' - 0"**
First Floor: **1,554 SQ. FT.**	Bedrooms: **4**	Depth: **67' - 0"**
Second Floor: **1,130 SQ. FT.**	Bathrooms: **2 1/2**	Foundation: **SLAB**

© The Sater Design Collection, Inc.

Second Floor

Plan:
HPK1500195

Style:
CRAFTSMAN

First Floor:
1,790 SQ. FT.

Second Floor:
860 SQ. FT.

Total:
2,650 SQ. FT.

Bedrooms:
3

Bathrooms:
2 ¹/₂

Width:
41' - 8"

Depth:
71' - 2"

Foundation:
SLAB

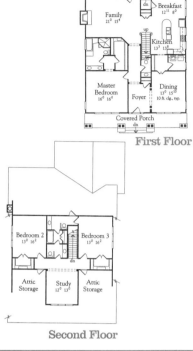

First Floor

Second Floor

Plan:
HPK1500196

Style:
COUNTRY COTTAGE

Square Footage:
1,698

Bedrooms:
3

Bathrooms:
2

Width:
51' - 8"

Depth:
49' - 8"

Foundation:
UNFINISHED BASEMENT

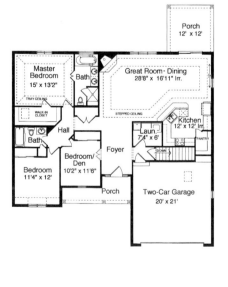

Plan:
HPK1500325

Style:
TRADITIONAL

First Floor:
1,503 SQ. FT.

Second Floor:
516 SQ. FT.

Total:
2,019 SQ. FT.

Bedrooms:
3

Bathrooms:
2 ¹/₂

Width:
43' - 4"

Depth:
60' - 8"

Featuring a lovely columned, covered porch by the entrance, the exterior of this home shows off tasteful detailing in its brick facade and window design. The garage is 23 square feet, but allows for an additional three-car capacity. Tray ceilings distinguish the dining room and eating area on the first floor, as well as in two of the bedrooms. The great room is dominated by a two-story cathedral ceiling. On cold nights, you'll savor the view as you nestle with your loved ones in front of the expansive fireplace. The kitchen is ideally configured with open access to the eating area, and more controlled proximity to the formal dining room. Plenty of closet space, two-and-a-half baths, and a large utility room cap off this stylish residence.

First Floor

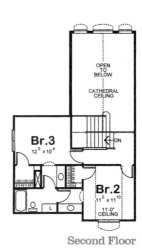

Second Floor

Plan:
HPK1500197

Style:
VICTORIAN

First Floor:
805 SQ. FT.

Second Floor:
779 SQ. FT.

Total:
1,584 SQ. FT.

Bedrooms:
3

Bathrooms:
1 ¹/₂

Width:
25' - 0"

Depth:
36' - 0"

Foundation:
**UNFINISHED
BASEMENT**

With pyramidal roofs, covered balcony, and frieze detailing, this 1,584-square-foot home borrows beauty from centuries past. Ideal for a narrow lot, the plan hosts a convenient first-level half-bath, open family and dining area, and kitchen with airy breakfast nook. The second level features a boudoir-style master suite with huge walk-in closet, spacious bath, and two charming bedrooms.

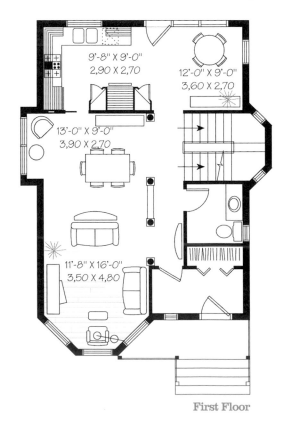

First Floor

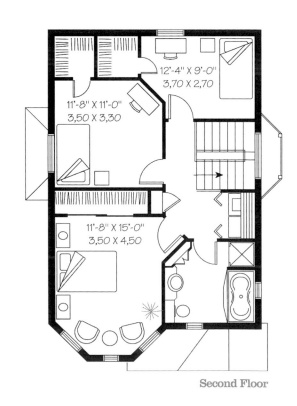

Second Floor

Plan:
HPK1500198

Style:
CRAFTSMAN

First Floor:
1,106 SQ. FT.

Second Floor:
1,010 SQ. FT.

Total:
2,116 SQ. FT.

Bonus Space:
200 SQ. FT.

Bedrooms:
3

Bathrooms:
2 1/2

Width:
37' - 6"

Depth:
54' - 0"

Foundation:
SLAB

An appealing Craftsman home dresses up any neighborhood. A deep porch anchored by heavy pilasters is an inviting spot for friends and family. The entry gallery introduces a layout that is open and defines spaces with decorative columns and wall breaks. The dining area looks out onto the front yard and enjoys a view of the fireplace in the gathering room. The island kitchen provides plenty of counter and cabinet space. A sunroom doubles as a breakfast area and has front-porch access. Two family bedrooms share a full bath on the second floor. The master suite features a large walk-in closet and super bath. An optional bonus room completes this space.

This home, as shown in photographs, may differ from the actual blueprints. For more detailed information, please check the floor plans carefully.

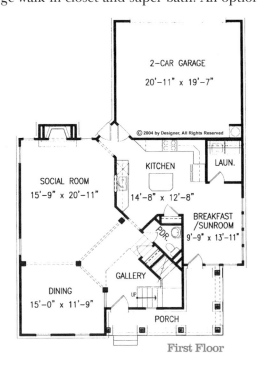

First Floor

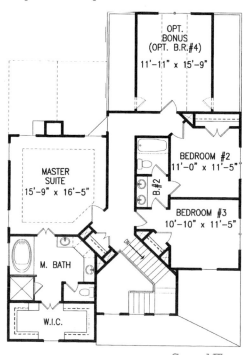

Second Floor

Plan:
HPK1500199

Style:
CRAFTSMAN

First Floor:
1,457 SQ. FT.

Second Floor:
1,185 SQ. FT.

Total:
2,642 SQ. FT.

Bedrooms:
3

Bathrooms:
2 ¹/2

Width:
38' - 0"

Depth:
52' - 0"

Foundation:
SLAB

Traditional neighborhood home design is captured in this home. Craftsman details with a modern layout anchor past and present to offer a comfortable family design. The foyer introduces the parlor—perfect spot to welcome guests—which sits off the open kitchen with snack bar. A morning room transitions the kitchen space to a large social room with built-ins and a fireplace. A formal dining room is just to the right of the kitchen. Upstairs, the master suite is framed by double doors and offers a lovely sitting area that opens to a covered porch. Two secondary bedrooms and a full bath complete this floor.

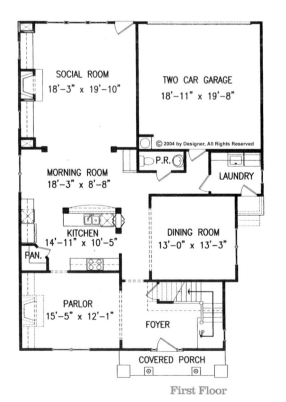

First Floor

Second Floor

Photo courtesy of Garrell Associates, Inc.
This home, as shown in photographs, may differ from the actual blueprints.

© WILLIAM E POOLE DESIGNS, INC.

Plan:
HPK1500326

Style:
NEOCLASSIC

First Floor:
3,545 SQ. FT.

Second Floor:
2,019 SQ. FT.

Total:
5,564 SQ. FT.

Bonus Space:
928 SQ. FT.

Bedrooms:
4

Bathrooms:
4 1/2 + 1/2

Width:
124' - 4"

Depth:
79' - 3"

Foundation:
CRAWLSPACE, UNFINISHED BASEMENT

This home provides a breathtaking example of the Neoclassical tradition. An impressive entrance is formed by an arched porch, fanned stairway, and columns. Upper and lower balconies, shuttered Palladian windows, a Widow's walk, and a side-loading garage lend the exterior of this home its grandeur. The interior is replete with more columns, as well as tray ceilings, an indoor balcony, built-in cabinets and desks, and an entertainment center. The formal dining room comes with butler's pantry, and leads directly off of the foyer for late-arriving dinner guests. A gallery and master study lead off in the opposite direction. The master suite of the main level holds a fireplace with private patio and deck access. Upstairs, find both front and sunset viewing decks. Three split bedrooms, and special storage space round out the surprise of the upper floor.

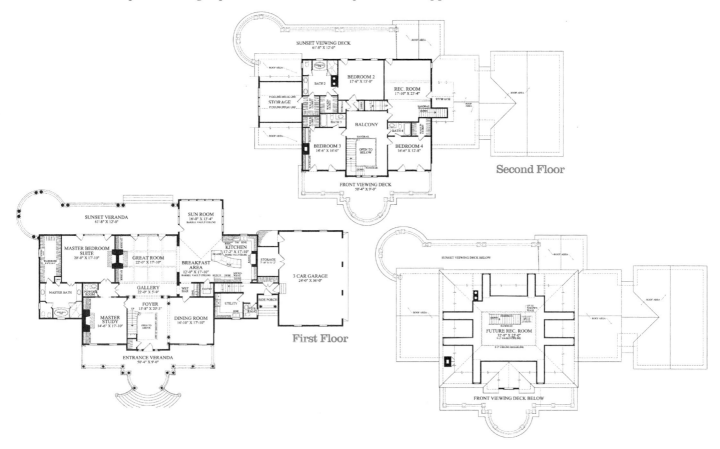

Second Floor

First Floor

325 New Home Plans
Homes with Historic Inspiration

Plan: HPK1500200

Style:
FRENCH

First Floor:
1,807 SQ. FT.

Second Floor:
1,970 SQ. FT.

Total:
3,777 SQ. FT.

Bedrooms:
4

Bathrooms:
3 1/2

Width:
57' - 4"

Depth:
53' - 6"

Foundation:
UNFINISHED WALKOUT BASEMENT

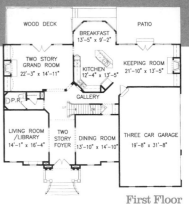

First Floor

Second Floor

Photo courtesy of Garrell Associates, Inc.
This home as shown in photographs may differ from the actual blueprints.

Plan: HPK1500201

First Floor

Second Floor

Style:
GEORGIAN

First Floor:
2,798 SQ. FT.

Second Floor:
1,496 SQ. FT.

Total:
4,294 SQ. FT.

Bonus Space:
515 SQ. FT.

Bedrooms:
4

Bathrooms:
3 1/2

Width:
91' - 10"

Depth:
57' - 2"

Foundation:
CRAWLSPACE, UNFINISHED BASEMENT

Plan:
HPK1500202

Style:
CRAFTSMAN

First Floor:
1,659 SQ. FT.

Second Floor:
1,290 SQ. FT.

Total:
2,949 SQ. FT.

Bonus Space:
463 SQ. FT.

Bedrooms:
4

Bathrooms:
3 1/2

Width:
43' - 4"

Depth:
82' - 0"

Foundation:
UNFINISHED BASEMENT

The stately brick facade evokes a timeless design. Once inside, formal living areas give way to the open floor plan, great for family interaction and entertaining. A side deck extends the living space outdoors. A rear staircase leads to a media room housed over the garage. A second stairwell accesses the remainder of the second floor, including the master suite and two family bedrooms separated by a Jack-and-Jill bath. Extra storage space in the garage is an added bonus.

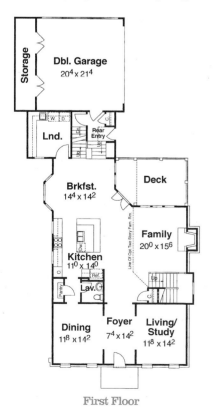

First Floor

Second Floor

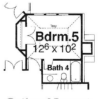

Optional Layout

Plan:
HPK1500203

Style:
SOUTHERN COLONIAL

First Floor:
2,670 SQ. FT.

Second Floor:
1,795 SQ. FT.

Total:
4,465 SQ. FT.

Bonus Space:
744 SQ. FT.

Bedrooms:
5

Bathrooms:
4 1/2 + 1/2

Width:
74' - 8"

Depth:
93' - 10"

Foundation:
CRAWLSPACE, UNFINISHED BASEMENT

© William E. Poole Designs, Inc.

A stately brick plantation home, this plan presents all the luxuries that are so desired by today's homeowner. Enter past the columned portico to the formal two-story foyer. To the left is a library with a corner fireplace; to the right, the dining room flows into an enormous kitchen, outfitted with an island serving bar. Exposed wood-beam ceilings in the kitchen, breakfast area, and family room add a vintage element. The master suite is a romantic hideaway, with a corner fireplace, whirlpool tub, and seated shower. Upstairs, four well-appointed bedrooms join a lounge area to finish the plan. Future space above the three-car garage is limited only by your imagination.

First Floor

Second Floor

© The Sater Design Collection, Inc.

Plan:
HPK1500204

Style:
COUNTRY COTTAGE

First Floor:
2,705 SQ. FT.

Second Floor:
1,241 SQ. FT.

Total:
3,946 SQ. FT.

Bedrooms:
4

Bathrooms:
4

Width:
98' - 0"

Depth:
60' - 0"

Foundation:
CRAWLSPACE, SLAB

Clapboard siding and a standing-seam roof set off this cottage elevation—a comfortable seaside retreat with an easygoing style. A central turret anchors a series of varied gables and rooflines, evoking the charm of Caribbean style. Square columns and a spare balustrade define the perimeter of a spacious entry porch, which leads to a gallery-style foyer. Pocket doors seclude a forward study featuring a step ceiling and views of the front property. An open arrangement of the formal rooms progresses into the plan without restrictions, bounded only by wide views of the outdoors. Retreating glass doors permit the living and dining spaces to extend to the veranda. Upstairs, the master suite adjoins a spare room that could serve as a study and leads out to a rear deck.

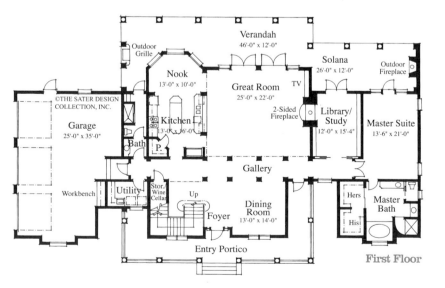

First Floor

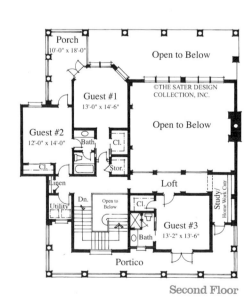

Second Floor

Plan:
HPK1500205

Style:
TRADITIONAL

First Floor:
2,811 SQ. FT.

Second Floor:
1,246 SQ. FT.

Total:
4,057 SQ. FT.

Bedrooms:
5

Bathrooms:
4 1/2

Width:
66' - 1"

Depth:
75' - 7"

Foundation:
CRAWLSPACE, SLAB, UNFINISHED BASEMENT

First Floor

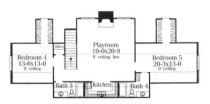

Second Floor

Plan:
HPK1500206

Style:
GOTHIC REVIVAL

Square Footage:
2,402

Bonus Space:
294 SQ. FT.

Bedrooms:
4

Bathrooms:
2 1/2

Width:
56' - 6"

Depth:
82' - 0"

Foundation:
CRAWLSPACE, SLAB, UNFINISHED BASEMENT

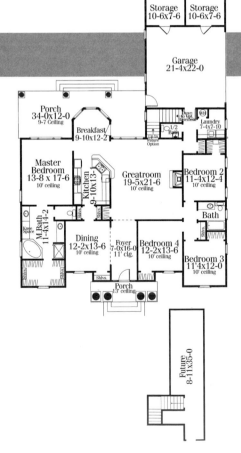

© William E. Poole Designs, Inc.

Plan:
HPK1500207

Style:
GREEK REVIVAL

First Floor:
2,337 SQ. FT.

Second Floor:
1,016 SQ. FT.

Total:
3,353 SQ. FT.

Bonus Space:
394 SQ. FT.

Bedrooms:
4

Bathrooms:
3 ¹/₂

Width:
66' - 2"

Depth:
71' - 2"

Foundation:
CRAWLSPACE

With an abundance of natural light and amenities, this home is sure to please. The sunporch doubles as a delightful area to enjoy meals with a view. A mud room off the utility room accesses a side porch and serves as a place to hang coats or shed dirty shoes before entering the kitchen or family room. The master bedroom, family room, and living room/library each boast a private fireplace. Upstairs houses three additional bedrooms, two sharing a full bath and one with an attached full bath. Future expansion space completes the second floor. Extra storage space in the garage is an added convenience.

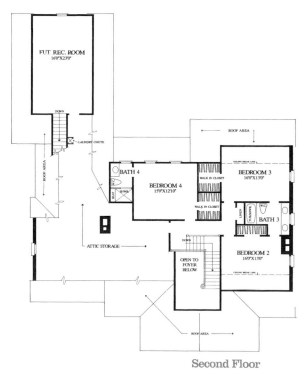

First Floor

Second Floor

Plan:
HPK1500208

Style:
GREEK REVIVAL

First Floor:
2,449 SQ. FT.

Second Floor:
1,094 SQ. FT.

Total:
3,543 SQ. FT.

Bonus Space:
409 SQ. FT.

Bedrooms:
4

Bathrooms:
3 ¹/₂

Width:
89' - 0"

Depth:
53' - 10"

Foundation:
CRAWLSPACE

© William E. Poole Designs, Inc.

An impressive front porch coupled with charming twin dormers makes this home a delightful addition to any neighborhood. The sunroom doubles as a delightful area to enjoy meals, a view of the backyard, and gain access to the rear porch. The family room and living room/library each boast a private fireplace. Upstairs houses three additional bedrooms, two sharing a full bath with a dual-sink vanity and one with an attached full bath. Future expansion space and extra storage space complete the second floor.

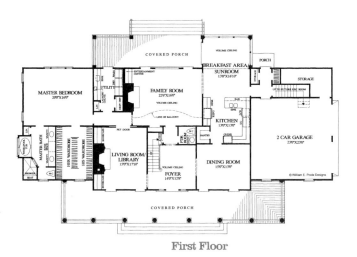

First Floor

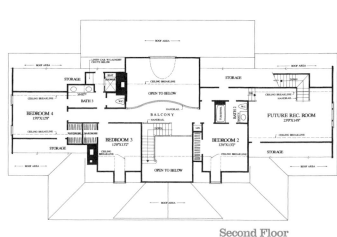

Second Floor

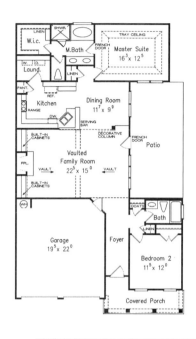

Plan:
HPK1500209

Style:
COUNTRY COTTAGE

Square Footage:
1,437

Bedrooms:
2

Bathrooms:
2

Width:
37' - 0"

Depth:
64' - 5"

Foundation:
SLAB

Plan:
HPK1500210

Style:
TRADITIONAL

Square Footage:
2,837

Bedrooms:
3

Bathrooms:
2 1/2

Width:
71' - 9"

Depth:
79' - 3"

Foundation:
CRAWLSPACE, SLAB, UNFINISHED BASEMENT

Plan:
HPK1500211

Style:
COUNTRY COTTAGE

Square Footage:
2,379

Bonus Space:
367 SQ. FT.

Bedrooms:
3

Bathrooms:
2 ¹/₂

Width:
61' - 0"

Depth:
81' - 9"

Foundation:
CRAWLSPACE, SLAB, UNFINISHED BASEMENT

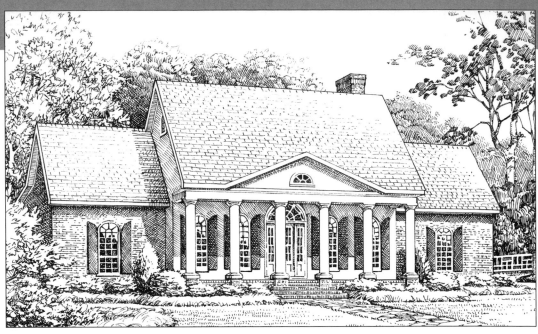

If you are looking for a home that grows with your family, this is it! Six rounded columns grace the front porch and lend a Colonial feel to this great home plan. Inside, the foyer opens to the formal dining space, which is only a few steps to the kitchen. A walk-in pantry, spacious counters and cabinets, snack bar, adjoining breakfast area, and planning desk make this kitchen efficient and gourmet. A private master suite features a sitting bay, twin walk-in closets, and an amenity-filled bath. Two oversized secondary bedrooms enjoy walk-in closets and share a corner bath. The entire second level is future space that will become exactly what you need. Plenty of storage can be found in the garage.

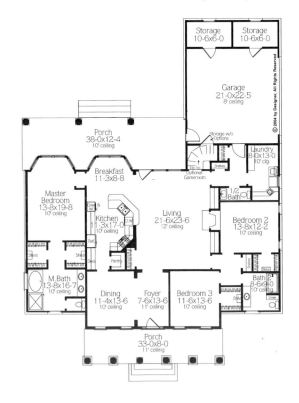

Optional Layout

Plan:
HPK1500212

First Floor

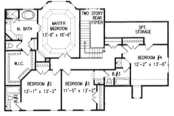

Second Floor

Style:
FARMHOUSE

First Floor:
1,602 SQ. FT.

Second Floor:
1,334 SQ. FT.

Total:
2,936 SQ. FT.

Bedrooms:
4

Bathrooms:
3 ¹/₂

Width:
54' - 0"

Depth:
45' - 8"

Foundation:
UNFINISHED WALKOUT BASEMENT

Plan:
HPK1500006

Style: **FARMHOUSE**	Bonus Space: **299 SQ. FT.**	Depth: **64' - 0"**
First Floor: **1,878 SQ. FT.**	Bedrooms: **4**	Foundation: **UNFINISHED WALKOUT BASEMENT, SLAB**
Second Floor: **826 SQ. FT.**	Bathrooms: **3 ¹/₂**	
Total: **2,704 SQ. FT.**	Width: **54' - 0"**	

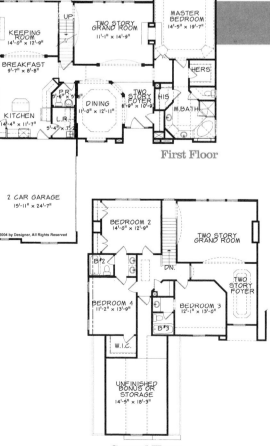

First Floor

Second Floor

© 2004 by Designer, All Rights Reserved

Plan:
HPK1500214

Style:
TRADITIONAL

First Floor:
1,803 SQ. FT.

Second Floor:
1,119 SQ. FT.

Total:
2,922 SQ. FT.

Bedrooms:
4

Bathrooms:
3

Width:
37' - 0"

Depth:
66' - 0"

Foundation:
CRAWLSPACE

First Floor

Second Floor

First Floor

Plan:
HPK1500215

Style:
COLONIAL

First Floor:
1,897 SQ. FT.

Second Floor:
777 SQ. FT.

Total:
2,674 SQ. FT.

Bonus Space:
705 SQ. FT.

Bedrooms:
4

Bathrooms:
4

Width:
55' - 0"

Depth:
49' - 0"

Foundation:
FINISHED BASEMENT

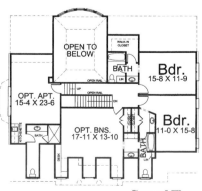

Second Floor

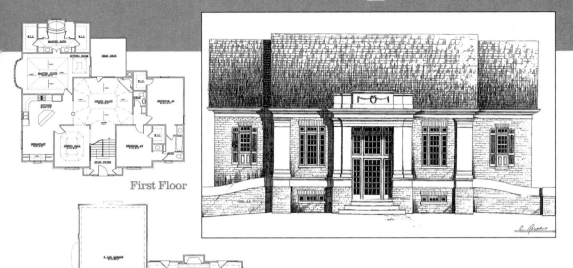

First Floor

Second Floor

Plan:
HPK1500216

Style:
TRADITIONAL

Square Footage:
1,831

Bedrooms:
3

Bathrooms:
3 1/2

Width:
54' - 0"

Depth:
51' - 0"

Foundation:
FINISHED WALKOUT BASEMENT

Plan:
HPK1500217

Style:
GEORGIAN

First Floor:
590 SQ. FT.

Second Floor:
925 SQ. FT.

Total:
1,515 SQ. FT.

Bedrooms:
3

Bathrooms:
2 1/2

Width:
48' - 0"

Depth:
30' - 0"

Foundation:
SLAB

First Floor

Second Floor

Plan:
HPK1500218

Style:
TRADITIONAL

First Floor:
1,498 SQ. FT.

Second Floor:
1,275 SQ. FT.

Total:
2,773 SQ. FT.

Bedrooms:
4

Bathrooms:
3 ½

Width:
63' - 0"

Depth:
38' - 2"

Foundation:
UNFINISHED BASEMENT

A brick facade with warm wood trim and flower boxes decorate the exterior of this home. Nine-foot ceilings on the first floor, a turned staircase with wood railing in the foyer, a direct-vent gas fireplace in the family room and multiple windows throughout the home create a beautiful interior. A laundry room, half bath, large closet, and built-in desk provide a wonderfully organized entry from the garage. An open kitchen and a breakfast alcove offer a spacious area for food preparation and service. A second-floor balcony overlooks the staircase and leads to a master bedroom suite with a luxurious bath with dual-sink vanity, whirlpool tub, and shower enclosure. Three additional bedrooms complete this family-sized home.

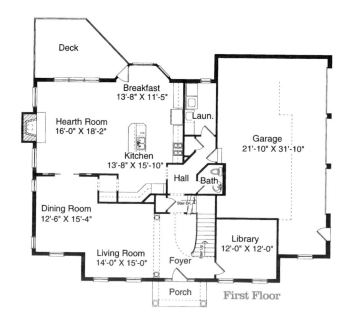

First Floor

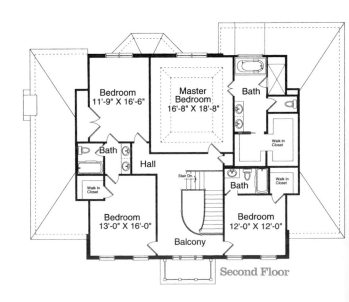

Second Floor

Plan:
HPK1500219

Style:
FARMHOUSE

First Floor:
1,725 SQ. FT.

Second Floor:
1,248 SQ. FT.

Total:
2,973 SQ. FT.

Bonus Space:
406 SQ. FT.

Bedrooms:
4

Bathrooms:
3 1/2

Width:
46' - 0"

Depth:
85' - 0"

Foundation:
CRAWLSPACE, SLAB

Southern charm can be seen throughout this farmhouse design. A wrapping porch is accessed by the dining room, the kitchen, and through the vaulted foyer. The family room is embellished with a coffered ceiling and fireplace. The kitchen provides a snack bar and breakfast nook. The first-floor master suite accommodates privacy and is outfitted with a full bath with dual-sink vanity and a walk-in closet. Upstairs, three family bedrooms share two full baths and a spacious recreation room. A third floor houses bonus space that can be completed as another bedroom suite.

First Floor

Second Floor

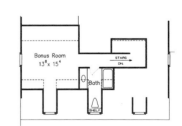

Plan:
HPK1500220

Style:
TRADITIONAL

First Floor:
1,720 SQ. FT.

Second Floor:
851 SQ. FT.

Total:
2,571 SQ. FT.

Bedrooms:
3

Bathrooms:
3

Width:
67' - 0"

Depth:
44' - 0"

Foundation:
CRAWLSPACE

Georgian influences create a formal and regal facade on this home. Inside, an open study and dining room sit to either side of the two-story foyer. A beautiful staircase leads the eye to the second floor, which provides two family bedrooms and a loft with skylights. Casual dining is a breeze in the breakfast bay. The kitchen features an eating bar and is near the laundry room and home office. A vaulted living room is enhanced by a fireplace, built-ins, rear-deck access, and a wall of windows. Convenient and secluded, the first-floor master suite includes a private bath and walk-in closet.

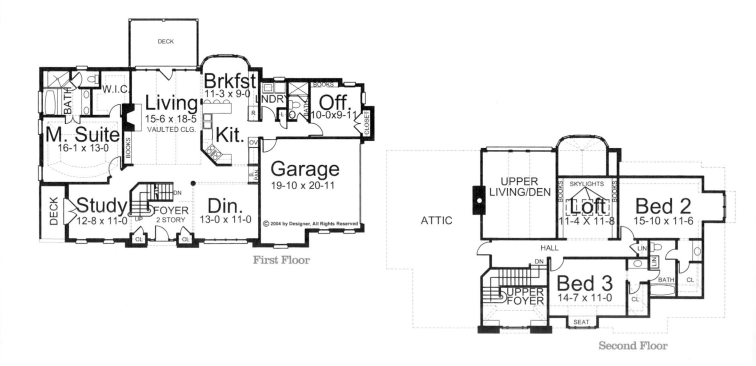

First Floor

Second Floor

© 2004 by Designer, All Rights Reserved

© William E. Poole Designs, Inc.

Plan:
HPK1500327

Style:
COLONIAL

First Floor:
1,785 SQ. FT.

Second Floor:
1,398 SQ. FT.

Total:
3,183 SQ. FT.

Bonus Space:
553 SQ. FT.

Bedrooms:
4

Bathrooms:
3

Width:
61' - 0"

Depth:
46' - 0"

Foundation:
CRAWLSPACE

A columned, arched portico and shuttered windows characterize this Colonial. You will be greeted once inside by a two-story foyer. The kitchen features a walk-in pantry, island, and breakfast nook. Bathroom #3 is conveniently centrally located between the study and breakfast nook. The left wing of this plan contains storage, a two-car garage, utility room and 20' x 15' family room. As if upstairs did not hold enough surprises (the master suite, two more bedrooms, and a view to below), a 17' x 26' bonus room will make an excellent recreation room.

First Floor

Second Floor

Plan:
HPK1500221

Style:
FRENCH

First Floor:
3,168 SQ. FT.

Second Floor:
998 SQ. FT.

Total:
4,166 SQ. FT.

Bonus Space:
210 SQ. FT.

Bedrooms:
4

Bathrooms:
3 ¹/₂

Width:
90' - 0"

Depth:
63' - 5"

Foundation:
SLAB, UNFINISHED BASEMENT, CRAWLSPACE

Stucco corner quoins, multiple gables, and graceful columns all combine to give this European manor plenty of appeal. Inside, a gallery entry presents a formal dining room on the right, defined by elegant columns, while the formal living room awaits just ahead. The highly efficient kitchen features a worktop island, pantry, and a serving bar to the nearby octagonal breakfast area. The family room offers a built-in entertainment center, a fireplace, and its own covered patio. The left side of the first floor is dedicated to the master suite. Here, the homeowner is pampered with an octagonal study, huge walk-in closet, lavish bath, and a very convenient nursery. The second floor contains two family bedrooms, each with a walk-in closet, and a media area with built-in bookshelves.

First Floor

Second Floor

Plan:
HPK1500222

Style:
EUROPEAN COTTAGE

First Floor:
4,252 SQ. FT.

Second Floor:
2,562 SQ. FT.

Total:
6,814 SQ. FT.

Bedrooms:
5

Bathrooms:
5 1/2 + 1/2

Width:
143' - 0"

Depth:
86' - 11"

Foundation:
SLAB

The grand entrance to this elegant European-style home is flanked by window bays stacked two high. The two-story foyer opens immediately to a formal dining room and a study; straight ahead is the entry to the living room and a magnificent curved staircase to the second level. An opulent master suite, filled with amenities, is located on the main floor; three more bedrooms, two baths, a game room, and an immense storage area are upstairs. A three-car garage and guest house can be reached by a covered walk.

This home, as shown in photographs, may differ from the actual blueprints. For more detailed information, please check the floor plans carefully.

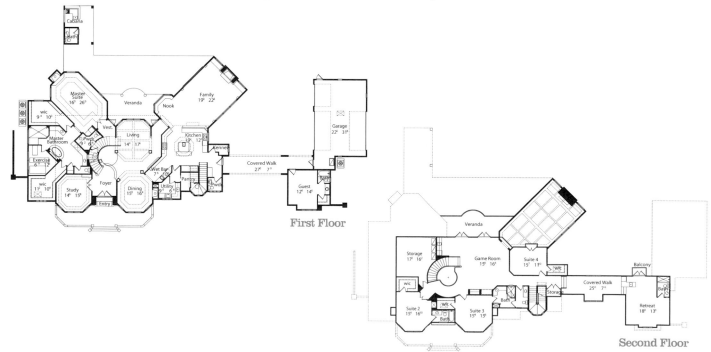

First Floor

Second Floor

Plan:
HPK1500223

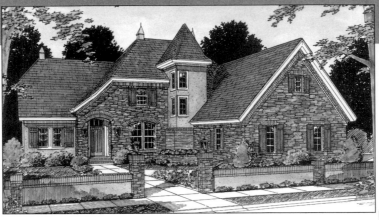

First Floor

Second Floor

Style:
EUROPEAN COTTAGE

First Floor:
2,014 SQ. FT.

Second Floor:
573 SQ. FT.

Total:
2,587 SQ. FT.

Bonus Space:
420 SQ. FT.

Bedrooms:
4

Bathrooms:
3

Width:
56' - 0"

Depth:
71' - 0"

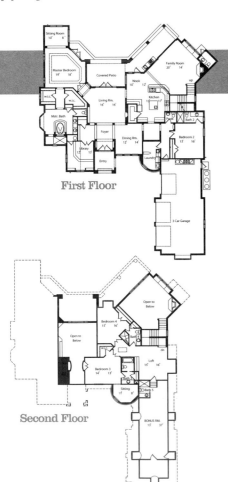

First Floor

Second Floor

Plan:
HPK1500224

Style:
EUROPEAN COTTAGE

First Floor:
3,526 SQ. FT.

Second Floor:
1,143 SQ. FT.

Total:
4,669 SQ. FT.

Bedrooms:
4

Bathrooms:
4

Width:
84' - 2"

Depth:
109' - 1"

Foundation:
SLAB

Plan:
HPK1500225

Style:
FRENCH COUNTRY

First Floor:
2,507 SQ. FT.

Second Floor:
1,472 SQ. FT.

Total:
3,979 SQ. FT.

Bedrooms:
3

Bathrooms:
3 1/2

Width:
59' - 6"

Depth:
82' - 8"

Foundation:
CRAWLSPACE

French and Tudor design elements delight the exterior with intriguing rooflines, surface materials, and window placement. The entry portico sits next to a stunning spiral-staircase tower and well-appointed, private study. Built-ins line the walls of the library/dining space, which is effeciently serves by the butler's pantry. The glorious counter, cabinet, and pantry space offered by the kitchen is further extended to a planning office. A first-floor master suite features a bumped-out alcove, full baths, and twin walk-in closets. Two family bedroom suites share a library with built-ins, a loft area, and a large bonus room with a balcony and wet bar.

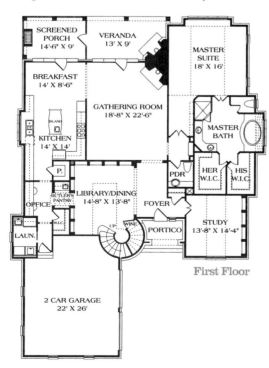

First Floor

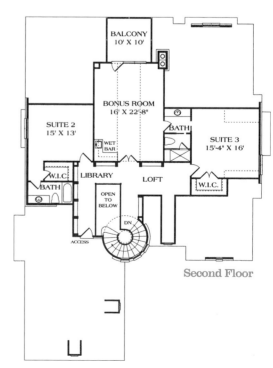

Second Floor

325 New Home Plans

English & Provencal Manors

Plan:
HPK1500226

Style:
FRENCH COUNTRY

First Floor:
2,423 SQ. FT.

Second Floor:
1,197 SQ. FT.

Total:
3,620 SQ. FT.

Bonus Space:
551 SQ. FT.

Bedrooms:
4

Bathrooms:
3 ¹/₂

Width:
56' - 6"

Depth:
97' - 3"

Foundation:
CRAWLSPACE

First Floor

Second Floor

Plan:
HPK1500227

Style:
FRENCH COUNTRY

First Floor:
1,833 SQ. FT.

Second Floor:
733 SQ. FT.

Total:
2,566 SQ. FT.

Bedrooms:
3

Bathrooms:
3

Width:
39' - 10"

Depth:
79' - 11"

Foundation:
SLAB

First Floor

Second Floor

ORDER BLUEPRINTS 24 HOURS, 7 DAYS A WEEK, AT 1-800-521-6797 OR EPLANS.COM

English & Provencal Manors

325 New Home Plans

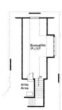

Plan:

HPK1500228

Style:
EUROPEAN COTTAGE

Square Footage:
2,559

Bonus Space:
324 SQ. FT.

Bedrooms:
3

Bathrooms:
2 ¹/₂

Width:
60' - 0"

Depth:
79' - 7"

Foundation:
SLAB

Plan:

HPK1500229

Style:
FRENCH COUNTRY

First Floor:
1,931 SQ. FT.

Second Floor:
768 SQ. FT.

Total:
2,699 SQ. FT.

Bonus Space:
220 SQ. FT.

Bedrooms:
4

Bathrooms:
3 ¹/₂

Width:
56' - 0"

Depth:
56' - 7"

Foundation:
SLAB

First Floor

Second Floor

Plan:
HPK1500230

Style:
FRENCH COUNTRY

First Floor:
3,229 SQ. FT.

Second Floor:
2,219 SQ. FT.

Total:
5,448 SQ. FT.

Bonus Space:
603 SQ. FT.

Bedrooms:
5

Bathrooms:
5 1/2 + 1/2

Width:
72' - 11"

Depth:
99' - 6"

Foundation:
CRAWLSPACE

Stone and stucco topped by varying roof lines and adorning a plan to be envied—this home is magnificent. Through the elegant portico and into the foyer, let your eye wander to the study on the right or the formal dining room on the left. Ahead you'll find a spacious family room joining with an open island kitchen and breakfast nook. The family room provides access to the covered lanai, which leads to a rear patio. The master suite and bath, two powder rooms, an office, and a laundry room complete this level—and there's another floor! Find four family bedrooms and private baths, a study, and space for a rec room upstairs.

Rear Exterior

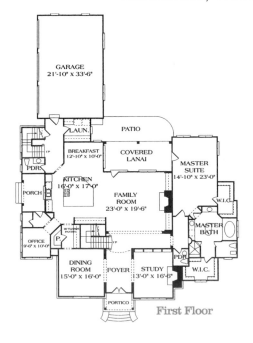

First Floor

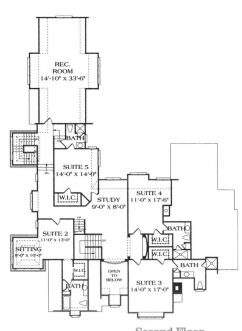

Second Floor

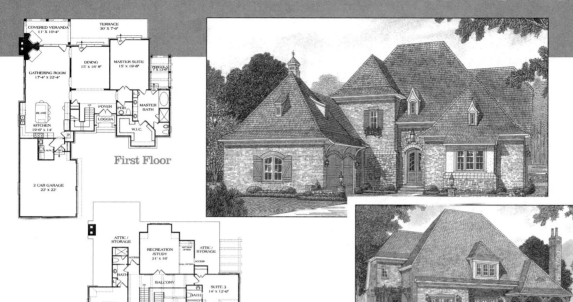

First Floor

COVERED VERANDA 11' X 10'-4"

TERRACE 30' X 7'-6"

DINING 15' X 16'-8"

MASTER SUITE 15' X 19'-8"

PERGOLA 7' X 13'-6"

GATHERING ROOM 17'-4" X 22'-4"

FOYER

POR.

MASTER BATH

LOGGIA

W.I.C.

KITCHEN 19'-6" X 14'

ISLAND

2 CAR GARAGE 22' X 22'

Second Floor

ATTIC / STORAGE

RECREATION /STUDY 21' X 16'

ATTIC / STORAGE

WET BAR OPTION

BATH

BALCONY

SUITE 3 14' X 12'-6"

SUITE 2 15' X 14'

BATH

W.I.C.

ATTIC / STORAGE

Rear Exterior

Plan:
HPK1500231

Style:
EUROPEAN COTTAGE

First Floor:
2,025 SQ. FT.

Second Floor:
1,310 SQ. FT.

Total:
3,335 SQ. FT.

Bedrooms:
3

Bathrooms:
3 ¹/₂

Width:
59' - 8"

Depth:
78' - 8"

Foundation:
CRAWLSPACE

Plan:
HPK1500232

Style: **FRENCH**	Total: **2,502 SQ. FT.**	Width: **42' - 0"**
First Floor: **2,148 SQ. FT.**	Bedrooms: **4**	Depth: **79' - 0"**
Second Floor: **354 SQ. FT.**	Bathrooms: **3**	Foundation: **SLAB**

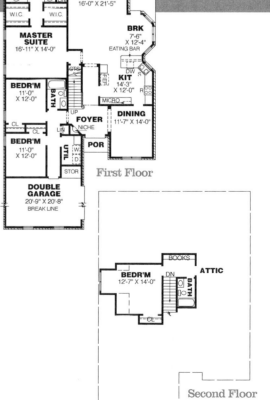

First Floor

MASTER BATH

F/P

GREAT ROOM 16'-0" X 21'-5"

POR

W.I.C.

W.I.C.

MASTER SUITE 16'-11" X 14'-0"

BRK 7'-6" X 12'-4"

EATING BAR

DW

KIT 14'-3" X 12'-0"

BEDR'M 11'-0" X 12'-0"

BATH

UP

MICRO

DINING 11'-7" X 14'-0"

FOYER

NICHE

CL

LIN

BEDR'M 11'-0" X 12'-0"

POR

UTIL

STOR

DOUBLE GARAGE 20'-9" X 20'-8"

BREAK LINE

BOOKS

BEDR'M 12'-7" X 14'-0"

DN

BATH

ATTIC

CL

Second Floor

Plan:
HPK1500233

Style:
FRENCH COUNTRY

Main Level:
1,703 SQ. FT.

Upper Level:
1,930 SQ. FT.

Lower Level:
1,233 SQ. FT.

Total:
4,866 SQ. FT.

Bedrooms:
4

Bathrooms:
4 1/2

Width:
67' - 0"

Depth:
58' - 0"

Foundation:
FINISHED WALKOUT BASEMENT

Rear Exterior

The arched recessed entry and stone and stucco facade combine to create the elegant exterior of this European-styled home. Inside, the study and formal dining room flank the foyer. The openness of the plan allows the fireplace in the expansive family room to warm the adjoining breakfast room and kitchen. The kitchen boasts an island snack bar, wraparound counters, and access to the screened porch. A utility area adjacent to the kitchen offers a mud room leading to the three-car garage. On the upper level, the luxurious master suite enjoys the view from a covered balcony. Three additional family bedrooms occupy the upper level along with two full baths. The lower level houses a recreation room with a fireplace, a guest suite/office, and a media room.

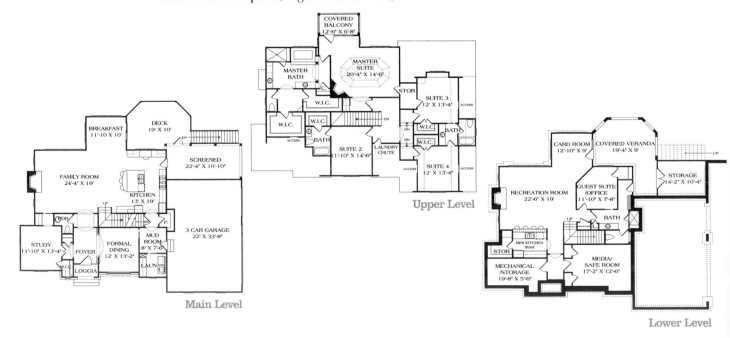

Main Level

Upper Level

Lower Level

Plan:
HPK1500234

Style:
FRENCH COUNTRY

Main Level:
1,805 SQ. FT.

Upper Level:
2,098 SQ. FT.

Lower Level:
1,393 SQ. FT.

Total:
5,296 SQ. FT.

Bedrooms:
5

Bathrooms:
4 1/2

Width:
62' - 2"

Depth:
54' - 0"

Foundation:
FINISHED WALKOUT BASEMENT

Three levels of European-style living includes all the perks of a modern, amenity-filled home. The first floor combines both formal spaces—dining room and study—and family spaces—family room, breakfast nook, and island kitchen. Each room is showered in natural light from banks of windows. The second level houses three family suites, a spacious study loft, and a magnificent master suite. The lower level focuses on entertainment and games. A huge home theater enjoys a wet bar for snacks and covered-lanai access. A large recreation room would make a great billiards hall. An additional guest suite and full bath complete this level.

Main Level

Upper Level

Lower Level

Plan:
HPK1500235

Style:
TRADITIONAL

Square Footage:
2,081

Bedrooms:
3

Bathrooms:
3

Width:
55' - 0"

Depth:
57' - 10"

Foundation:
CRAWLSPACE, SLAB

Alternate Exterior

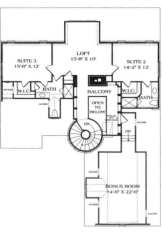

First Floor

Second Floor

Plan:
HPK1500236

Style: **FRENCH**	Total: **3,166 SQ. FT.**	Width: **50' - 8"**
First Floor: **1,980 SQ. FT.**	Bonus Space: **433 SQ. FT.**	Depth: **69' - 0"**
Second Floor: **1,186 SQ. FT.**	Bedrooms: **3**	Foundation: **CRAWLSPACE**
	Bathrooms: **3 1/2**	

Plan:
HPK1500237

Style:
FRENCH COUNTRY

Main Level:
2,563 SQ. FT.

Upper Level:
298 SQ. FT.

Lower Level:
1,870 SQ. FT.

Total:
4,731 SQ. FT.

Bonus Space:
532 SQ. FT.

Bedrooms:
3

Bathrooms:
3 1/2

Width:
84' - 2"

Depth:
89' - 3"

Foundation:
FINISHED WALKOUT BASEMENT

Arched gables and windows, a recessed entry, and varied rooflines complement the brick and stone facade of this French Country beauty. Inside, beyond the foyer, a generous gathering room with a fireplace awaits. The island kitchen features a breakfast nook, plenty of counter space, and access to a screened porch. Nearby, a utility area leads to the garage and a side porch. The master bedroom is privately tucked away on the right side of the plan, complete with a roomy walk-in closet, a garden tub, a separate shower, a compartmented toilet, dual vanities, and a sitting area that accesses the veranda. Downstairs houses two additional family bedrooms, each with a full bath and doors leading to the veranda. A wet bar and wine storage area make the recreation room a perfect place to entertain guests. The upper level harbors a fourth bedroom/bonus room, full bath, and study loft.

Rear Exterior

Main Level

Lower Level

Upper Level

Plan:
HPK1500238

Style:
FRENCH

Square Footage:
1,640

Bedrooms:
3

Bathrooms:
2

Width:
50' - 0"

Depth:
55' - 4"

Foundation:
SLAB

Plan:
HPK1500239

Style:
EUROPEAN COTTAGE

Square Footage:
1,810

Bedrooms:
3

Bathrooms:
2

Width:
67' - 8"

Depth:
45' - 0"

Foundation:
UNFINISHED BASEMENT

Plan:
HPK1500240

Style:
FRENCH

First Floor:
3,001 SQ. FT.

Second Floor:
1,263 SQ. FT.

Total:
4,264 SQ. FT.

Bedrooms:
4

Bathrooms:
5 ¹/₂

Width:
75' - 1"

Depth: 87' - 2"

Foundation:
SLAB

A first-floor master bedroom is quickly becoming a must-have for new home design, and this French-inspired design provides a wonderful suite. The master bath includes dual-sink vanities, a gorgeous soaking tub, and a separate shower. Another first-floor bedroom is great for guests, and there's a third bedroom upstairs, sharing the floor with an ultra-modern media room. The bumped-out breakfast room off the kitchen provides a circular wall of windows with views to the rear yard. Off the foyer you'll find the study and dining room, and straight ahead is the heart of the home, the hearth-warmed living room.

This home, as shown in photographs, may differ from the actual blueprints. For more detailed information, please check the floor plans carefully.

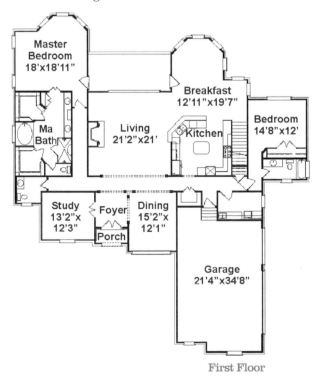

First Floor

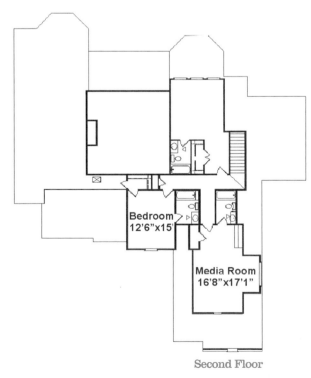

Second Floor

Plan:
HPK1500241

Style:
FRENCH

Square Footage:
2,544

Bedrooms:
3

Bathrooms:
2

Width:
60' - 6"

Depth:
74' - 4"

Foundation:
SLAB, CRAWLSPACE

Plan:
HPK1500242

Style:
FRENCH COUNTRY

Square Footage:
2,998

Bonus Space:
345 SQ. FT.

Bedrooms:
4

Bathrooms:
3 1/2

Width:
69' - 7"

Depth:
81' - 6"

Foundation:
SLAB

English & Provencal Manors

Plan:
HPK1500243

Style:
CONTEMPORARY

First Floor:
4,864 SQ. FT.

Second Floor:
1,215 SQ. FT.

Total:
6,079 SQ. FT.

Bonus Space:
854 SQ. FT.

Bedrooms:
5

Bathrooms:
5 1/2

Width:
133' - 0"

Depth:
63' - 0"

Foundation:
FINISHED WALKOUT BASEMENT

Introducing the finest in European Country estate designs; incredible exterior wood details, stone accents, and smooth stucco create an enchanting facade. Notable features such as the circular staircase, oval library, sequestered home theater, gourmet island kitchen with oversized walk-in pantry, and extensive amenities—including abundant closets—in the master suite create a haven of comfort and refinement. The second level houses two family bedrooms with private baths and walk-in closets, large bonus room with kitchen, and additional fully outfitted private living space for a live-in nanny.

This home, as shown in photographs, may differ from the actual blueprints. For more detailed information, please check the floor plans carefully.

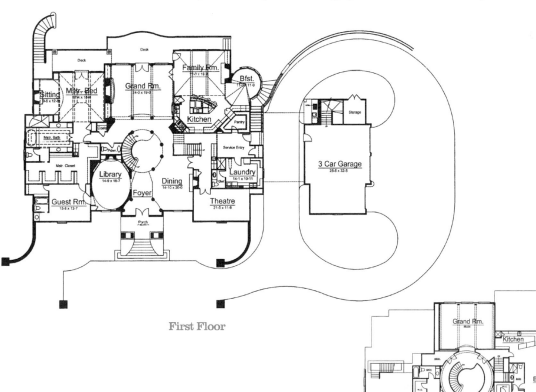

First Floor

Second Floor

325
New Home Plans

English & Provencal Manors

Plan:
HPK1500244

Style:
COUNTRY COTTAGE

Square Footage:
4,615

Bedrooms:
4

Bathrooms:
4 ½

Width:
109' - 10"

Depth:
89' - 4"

Foundation:
SLAB

Plan:
HPK1500245

Style:	Total:	Width:
COUNTRY COTTAGE	**3,774 SQ. FT.**	**58' - 1"**
	Bonus Space:	**Depth:**
First Floor:	**340 SQ. FT.**	**125' - 4"**
2,600 SQ. FT.	**Bedrooms:**	**Foundation:**
Second Floor:	**4**	**CRAWLSPACE**
1,174 SQ. FT.	**Bathrooms:**	
	4	

First Floor

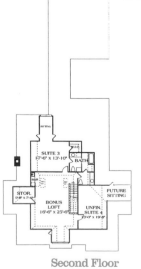

Second Floor

Plan:
HPK1500328

Style:
TRADITIONAL

Square Footage:
2,038

Bedrooms:
3

Bathrooms:
2

Width:
59' - 0"

Depth:
58' - 0"

Stone masonry, columns, and Palladian windows mark the exterior, with further surprises in store on the inside! An arched entry gives way to a planning area on the right, or the family room straight ahead. A snack bar separates the family room from the kitchen, and the latter from the dining area. A wonderful covered porch is accessible directly from the dining room. The bedrooms on the main level exist at opposite ends. The master bath boasts a sloped ceiling, double vanity, compartmented toilet and shower, and walk-in closet. The master bedroom features a tray ceiling. But wait until you see the upstairs: there's a patio, study, game room, exercise room and theater, plus a bar, and storage space galore.

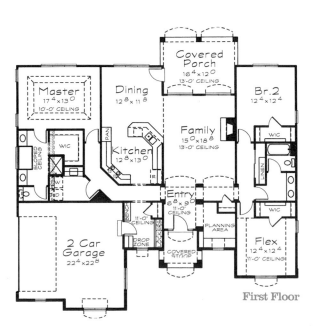

First Floor

Basement

Optional Layout

Plan:
HPK1500304

Style:
FRENCH COUNTRY

Square Footage:
2,255

Bedrooms:
2

Bathrooms:
2

Width:
53' - 0"

Depth:
78' - 0"

Lifted from the French countryside! Arched windows with wooden shutters meet stucco and stone masonry with wood framing to immerse you in your European Country cottage. Enter and discover a library with tray ceiling to house your treasured collection. Entertain in the great room on the main level or upstairs in your home theater, where you will also find the family room, kitchenette, third bedroom with full bath and walk-in closet, and extra storage. The master suite features His and Hers matching walk-in closets, and an enormous bathroom. The family bedroom on the main level has an extra-high ceiling. Off of the great room, there's a kitchen with center island, pantry and bar with an eating area leading directly onto a rear covered porch.

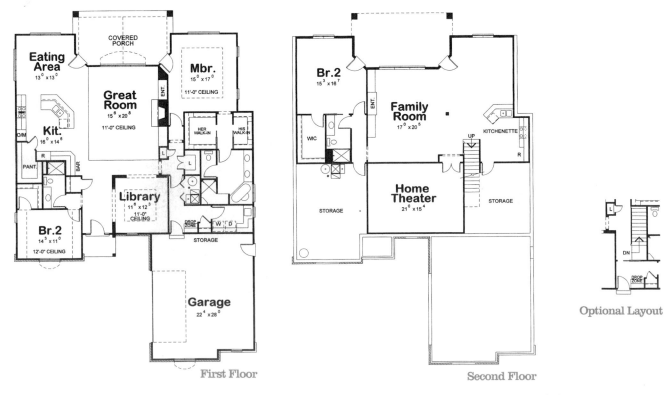

First Floor

Second Floor

Optional Layout

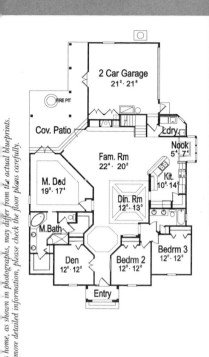

Plan:
HPK1500247

Style:
EUROPEAN CONTEMPORARY

Square Footage:
2,293

Bonus Space:
509 SQ. FT.

Bedrooms:
4

Bathrooms:
3

Width:
51' - 0"

Depth:
79' - 4"

Foundation:
SLAB

This home, as shown in photographs, may differ from the actual blueprints. For more detailed information, please check the floor plans carefully.

Plan:
HPK1500248

Style:
TRADITIONAL

Square Footage:
3,175

Bedrooms:
4

Bathrooms:
2 1/2

Width:
79' - 0"

Depth:
65' - 4"

Foundation:
CRAWLSPACE, UNFINISHED BASEMENT, SLAB

325
New Home Plans

English & Provencal Manors

Plan:
HPK1500249

Style:
FRENCH COUNTRY

First Floor:
3,337 SQ. FT.

Second Floor:
1,292 SQ. FT.

Total:
4,629 SQ. FT.

Bedrooms:
4

Bathrooms:
4 1/2

Width:
84' - 10"

Depth:
102' - 3"

First Floor

Second Floor

Plan:
HPK1500250

Style:	**Total:**	**Bathrooms:**
TRADITIONAL	**3,415 SQ. FT.**	**3 1/2**
First Floor:	**Bonus Space:**	**Width:**
2,329 SQ. FT.	**308 SQ. FT.**	**67' - 4"**
Second Floor:	**Bedrooms:**	**Depth:**
1,086 SQ. FT.	**4**	**78' - 8"**

First Floor

Second Floor

Plan:
HPK1500251

Style:
TRANSITIONAL

First Floor:
2,094 SQ. FT.

Second Floor:
874 SQ. FT.

Total:
2,968 SQ. FT.

Basement:
638 SQ. FT.

Bedrooms:
3

Bathrooms:
2 ¹/₂

Width:
61' - 6"

Depth:
72' - 8"

Foundation:
FINISHED WALKOUT BASEMENT

Indoor/outdoor relationships are really the defining characteristics of this transitional stone-and-stucco design. Positioned to take advantage of natural light, the sun room provides a great alternative to the lakeside dining room—and both are convenient to the island kitchen. The first-floor master suite provides access to the rear deck. Don't miss the His and Hers walk-in closets and sumptuous bath here, as well. Upstairs, the captain's quarters views not only the hearth-warmed gathering room, but also the rear deck. Two family bedrooms sharing a full bath round out this level.

This home, as shown in photographs, may differ from the actual blueprints. For more detailed information, please check the floor plans carefully.

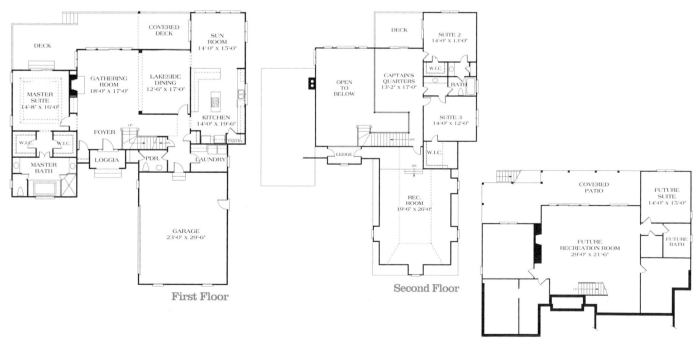

First Floor

Second Floor

Plan:
HPK1500252

Style:
FRENCH

First Floor:
2,556 SQ. FT.

Second Floor:
1,667 SQ. FT.

Total:
4,223 SQ. FT.

Bedrooms:
4

Bathrooms:
3 1/2 + 1/2

Width:
62' - 3"

Depth:
76' - 9"

First Floor

Second Floor

Plan:
HPK1500253

Style:
FRENCH

First Floor:
2,292 SQ. FT.

Second Floor:
1,010 SQ. FT.

Total:
3,302 SQ. FT.

Bonus Space:
278 SQ. FT.

Bedrooms:
4

Bathrooms:
3 1/2

Width:
75' - 0"

Depth:
72' - 8"

First Floor

Second Floor

Plan:
HPK1500254

Style:
FRENCH COUNTRY

First Floor:
1,805 SQ. FT.

Second Floor:
2,096 SQ. FT.

Total:
3,901 SQ. FT.

Basement:
1,414 SQ. FT.

Bedrooms:
5

Bathrooms:
4 1/2

Width:
62' - 2"

Depth:
54' - 0"

Foundation:
FINISHED WALKOUT BASEMENT

The stone and stucco facades gives this home a distinctly European flavor, and the arches atop the portico, dormers, and first-floor windows give it grace. A practical floor plan is revealed once inside, with living areas on the main level, bedrooms upstairs, and fun and games in the basement. The island kitchen is a dream, with miles of prep space and close proximity to a cozy breakfast area. The family room and rec room each offer gorgeous fireplaces. Guests staying in the lower-level bedroom know they're in for a good time with the billiards room and bar nearby. A huge garage and plenty of storage inside round out the practicality of this design.

325
New Home Plans

English & Provencal Manors

Plan:
HPK1500255

Style:
EUROPEAN COTTAGE

Main Level:
1,805 SQ. FT.

Upper Level:
2,084 SQ. FT.

Lower Level:
1,414 SQ. FT.

Total:
5,303 SQ. FT.

Bedrooms:
5

Bathrooms:
4 1/2

Width:
62' - 2"

Depth:
54' - 0"

Foundation:
FINISHED WALKOUT BASEMENT

Rear Exterior

Reminiscent of the European countryside, this cottage encorporates stucco and stone to great visual effect. With three levels of living, everyone will have a favorite room. The lower level incorporates a billiards room, a rec room, and storage with a guest space—but a teenager would probably fit just as well. Living spaces are on the main level and include a gorgeous island kitchen, spacious hearth-warmed family room, and an elegant dining room near the study. Bedrooms—each with a walk-in closet—and full baths are located on the upper level. The master bath will take your breath away.

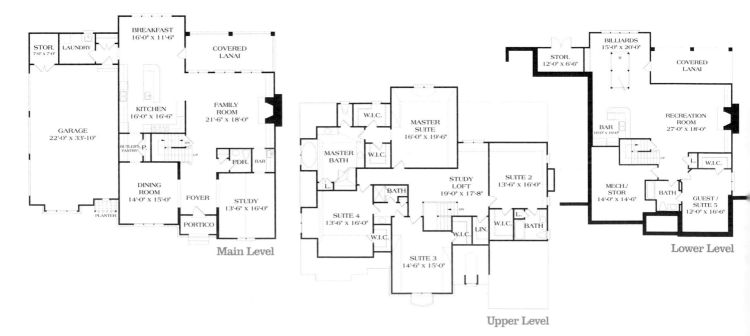

Main Level

Upper Level

Lower Level

ORDER BLUEPRINTS 24 HOURS, 7 DAYS A WEEK, AT 1-800-521-6797 OR EPLANS.COM

Plan:
HPK1500256

Style:
MEDITERRANEAN

First Floor:
3,633 SQ. FT.

Second Floor:
695 SQ. FT.

Total:
4,328 SQ. FT.

Bedrooms:
5

Bathrooms:
5 1/2

Width:
115' - 7"

Depth:
109' - 8"

Foundation:
SLAB

Arched windows and a dramatic portico with scrolled columns are gracefully featured in this Mediterranean design. The foyer is just as expressive, with more scrolled columns and soft curves to match the arched doorway. Mosaic tiles on the floor and steps bring touches of color and polish to earth-toned surfaces. The master suite and bath with patio are to the right of the plan, while the guest rooms are to the left, near the family room and kitchen. A spacious lanai, here enclosed by a greenhouse, features a pool and spa lined with trees and other botanicals. Notice the wet bar, ready with cool drinks for visitors to this unexpected sanctuary.

This home, as shown in photographs, may differ from the actual blueprints. For more detailed information, please check the floor plans carefully.

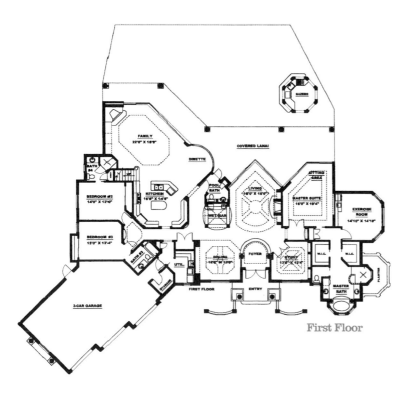

First Floor

Second Floor

Plan:
HPK1500257

Style:
ITALIANATE

Square Footage:
3,271

Bedrooms:
4

Bathrooms:
3 1/2

Width:
74' - 8"

Depth:
118' - 0"

Foundation:
SLAB

© The Sater Design Collection, Inc.

©THE SATER DESIGN COLLECTION, INC.

Plan:
HPK1500258

Style:
ITALIANATE

Square Footage:
2,907

Width:
65' - 0"

Bedrooms:
3

Bathrooms:
2 1/2

Depth:
84' - 0"

Foundation:
SLAB

©THE SATER DESIGN COLLECTION, INC.

Photo by CJ Walker.
This home, as shown in photographs, may differ from the actual blueprints.

Plan:
HPK1500259

Style:
ITALIANATE

First Floor:
4,742 SQ. FT.

Second Floor:
1,531 SQ. FT.

Total:
6,273 SQ. FT.

Bedrooms:
4

Bathrooms:
4 $^{1}/_{2}$ + $^{1}/_{2}$

Width:
96' - 0"

Depth:
134' - 8"

Foundation:
SLAB

The majestic entrance is just the beginning to this magnificent estate. A short hallway to the right of the foyer leads into the master suite which comprises the entire right side of the plan downstairs. The master bath offers dual vanities, a large shower, and a tub with an enclosed view of a privacy garden. His and Her walk-in closets lead from the dressing area, which flows easily into the bedroom. Within the bedroom, a sitting room offers a quiet retreat. The left side of the plan belongs to a spacious gourmet kitchen with an island snack-bar, plenty of counter space, a breakfast nook, and a large leisure area. Adjacent to the kitchen is a guest bedroom with a private full bath. Upstairs there are two additional bedrooms, each with a full bath and walk-in closet, one with a balcony. A media room is the finishing touch on this masterpiece.

This home, as shown in photographs, may differ from the actual blueprints. For more detailed information, please check the floor plans carefully.

First Floor

Second Floor

Plan:
HPK1500260

Style:
ITALIANATE

First Floor:
1,868 SQ. FT.

Second Floor:
1,292 SQ. FT.

Total:
3,160 SQ. FT.

Bedrooms:
5

Bathrooms:
3 1/2

Width:
55' - 0"

Depth:
59' - 4"

Foundation:
SLAB

First Floor

Second Floor

First Floor

Plan:
HPK1500261

Style:
SPANISH COLONIAL

First Floor:
2,443 SQ. FT.

Second Floor:
1,212 SQ. FT.

Total:
3,655 SQ. FT.

Bedrooms:
5

Bathrooms:
3 1/2

Width:
71' - 0"

Depth:
77' - 4"

Foundation:
SLAB

Second Floor

Plan:
HPK1500262

Style:
ITALIANATE

First Floor:
5,265 SQ. FT.

Second Floor:
746 SQ. FT.

Total:
6,011 SQ. FT.

Bedrooms:
4

Bathrooms:
4 1/2

Width:
99' - 4"

Depth:
140' - 0"

Foundation:
SLAB

Passing the courtyard and beautifully arched entry, visitors will marvel at the intersecting foyer, which leads ahead to the living room and connects the left and right wings of the plan. The dining room and study flank the entryway, establishing the home's formal spaces. Ahead, the living room features one of the home's several fireplaces and a row of accent windows placed just below the astonishing 22-foot ceiling. A dramatic array of windows frames the amazing view of the plan's garden lanai and pool. Two bedrooms at the left of the plan are attended by full baths and walk-in closets. But the star of the show is the resplendent master suite, which incorporates all the luxury amenities appropriate to a home of this magnitude.

Photo by Laurence Taylor Photography.
This home, as shown in photographs, may differ from the actual blueprints.
For more detailed information, please check the floor plans carefully.

First Floor

Second Floor

Plan:
HPK1500263

Style:
MEDITERRANEAN

First Floor:
5,060 SQ. FT.

Second Floor:
1,720 SQ. FT.

Total:
6,780 SQ. FT.

Bedrooms:
5

Bathrooms:
6

Width:
103' - 0"

Depth:
133' - 6"

Foundation:
SLAB

This award-winning two-story embraces many unique features. Entering through the stylish front steps and double entry doors provides a magnificent view of the pool area beyond the living room. A fireplace and built-in shelves grace one wall of the living room. The oversized family room features a built-in entertainment center and a second fireplace. The spacious master suite includes a large sitting area. The luxurious master bath features an oversized tub and a large dual-head shower area. Two huge walk-in closets and His and Her water closets complete this bathroom design. The study with built-in bookshelves, large guest bedroom suite, powder room, pool bath, utility room, and two separate two-car garages complete the first floor. Large pocket-sliders open to the covered lanai and outdoor kitchen area.

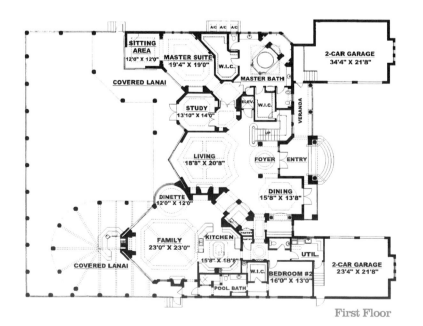

First Floor

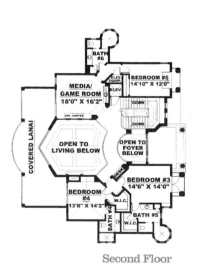

Second Floor

Photography by John Sciarrino, courtesy of Giovanni Photography.
This home, as shown in photographs, may differ from the actual blueprints.

Plan:
HPK1500264

Style:
MEDITERRANEAN

Square Footage:
3,370

Bonus Space:
630 SQ. FT.

Bedrooms:
3

Bathrooms:
3 ¹/₂

Width:
74' - 6"

Depth:
109' - 6"

Foundation:
SLAB

This stunning home home won the Parade of Homes award for Best Architectural Design. It features a unique balance of coziness and elegance. The floor plan flows flawlessly without compromising privacy or style. Natural views and outdoor living spaces enhance the open, spacious feeling inside this home. The overall layout and flow of the house and coffered ceilings maximize daylight while reflecting grandeur and richness. A pass-through wet bar may also be used as a butler's pantry. The loft above the garage is a fun and logical use of space for a second-floor game room or media room. The gourmet kitchen is superior in design and convenience. The dropped coffered ceiling in the kitchen provides intimate recessed lighting and a wonderful place to display art and kitchen decor.

This home, as shown in photographs, may differ from the actual blueprints. For more detailed information, please check the floor plans carefully.

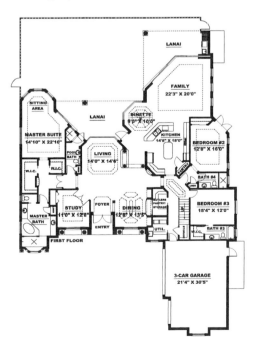

Plan:
HPK1500265

Style:
NW CONTEMPORARY

First Floor:
2,227 SQ. FT.

Second Floor:
771 SQ. FT.

Total:
2,998 SQ. FT.

Bedrooms:
4

Bathrooms:
4

Width:
58' - 8"

Depth:
68' - 0"

Foundation:
SLAB

First Floor

Second Floor

First Floor

Plan:
HPK1500266

Style:
MEDITERRANEAN

First Floor:
2,699 SQ. FT.

Second Floor:
1,006 SQ. FT.

Total:
3,705 SQ. FT.

Bedrooms:
4

Bathrooms:
5

Width:
65' - 0"

Depth:
95' - 0"

Foundation:
SLAB

Second Floor

Mediterranean & Spanish Styles

325
New Home Plans

Plan:
HPK1500267

Style:
CONTEMPORARY

First Floor:
4,257 SQ. FT.

Second Floor:
1,468 SQ. FT.

Total:
5,725 SQ. FT.

Bedrooms:
5

Bathrooms:
4

Width:
91' - 0"

Depth:
100' - 8"

Foundation:
SLAB

This home is classically Mediterranean, with its stucco facade, sprawling layout, and expansive rear view from within. Bedrooms have been split to the far sides of the first floor with three on the left—sharing a full bath, but with the pool bath nearby as well—and the master suite occupying the right wing. Living areas are clustered in the center, making gathering family and friends together for any occasion a breeze. A guest suite and game room are attractions on the second level, along with a spacious loft area.

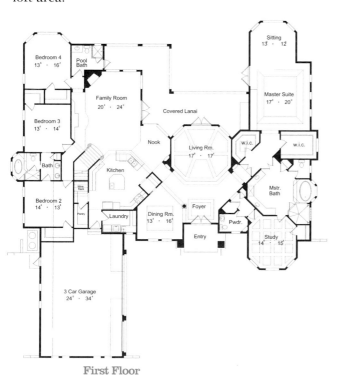

First Floor

Second Floor

Plan:
HPK1500268

Style:
MEDITERRANEAN

First Floor:
4,431 SQ. FT.

Second Floor:
989 SQ. FT.

Total:
5,420 SQ. FT.

Bedrooms:
5

Bathrooms:
5 1/2

Width:
105' - 7"

Depth:
100' - 4"

Foundation:
SLAB

Sprawling space, wide open rooms, and a flowing indoor/outdoor relationship are Mediterranean influences brought to life in this design. The covered rear porch includes a fireplace on one end and an outdoor kitchen at the other. The home is filled with appealing atmosphere, varying throughout with a variety of ceiling treatments. A split-bedroom design works wonders here as the master suite and to-die-for master bath encompass the entire left wing, leaving the right side to two family bedrooms with private baths and a game room. Another bed and bath, the home theater, and a meditation room reside on the second level. Enough storage for out-of-season decorations and clothing is also available.

Second Floor

First Floor

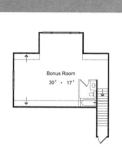

Bonus Room
30' · 17'

Plan:
HPK1500269

Style:
TRADITIONAL

Square Footage:
2,716

Bonus Space:
696 SQ. FT.

Bedrooms:
4

Bathrooms:
3

Width:
96' - 10"

Depth:
54' - 8"

Foundation:
SLAB

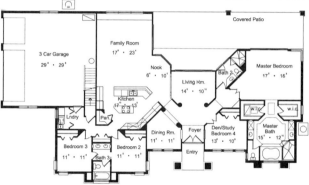

Plan:
HPK1500270

Style:
FLORIDIAN

Square Footage:
2,447

Bedrooms:
4

Bathrooms:
3

Width:
93' - 0"

Depth:
50' - 0"

Foundation:
SLAB

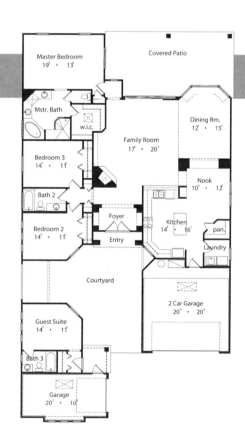

Plan:
HPK1500271

Style:
CONTEMPORARY

Square Footage:
2,052

Bedrooms:
3

Bathrooms:
3

Width:
60' - 0"

Depth:
50' - 0"

Foundation:
SLAB

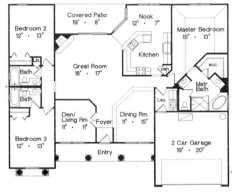

Plan:
HPK1500272

Style:
MEDITERRANEAN

Square Footage:
2,581

Width:
60' - 0"

Bedrooms:
4

Bathrooms:
3

Depth:
75' - 0"

Foundation:
SLAB

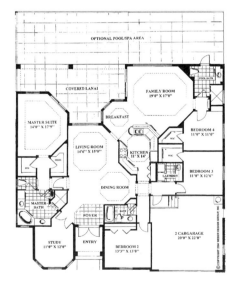

Mediterranean & Spanish Styles

325
New Home Plans

Plan:
HPK1500273

Style:
MEDITERRANEAN

First Floor:
1,500 SQ. FT.

Second Floor:
3,187 SQ. FT.

Total:
4,687 SQ. FT.

Basement:
1,000 SQ. FT.

Bedrooms:
4

Bathrooms:
4 ¹/₂

Width:
85' - 4"

Depth:
90' - 10"

Foundation:
UNFINISHED WALKOUT BASEMENT

Rear Exterior

Situated below the gorgeous roof with a covered front porch supported by stately pillars, this Mediterranean beauty is three levels of luxury. A guest suite with full bath occupies the lower level, a prime location to take advantage of the exercise and game rooms. The main level is masterfully laid out: an extraordinary kitchen, breakfast room, and wet bar are to the far left; the master suite and bath are nestled to the far right; and the center of the home offers the grand room, dining room, and study for your enjoyment. Upstairs are the kids' play room, bedrooms, and baths, along with amazing views of the two-story rooms below.

This home, as shown in photographs, may differ from the actual blueprints. For more detailed information, please check the floor plans carefully.

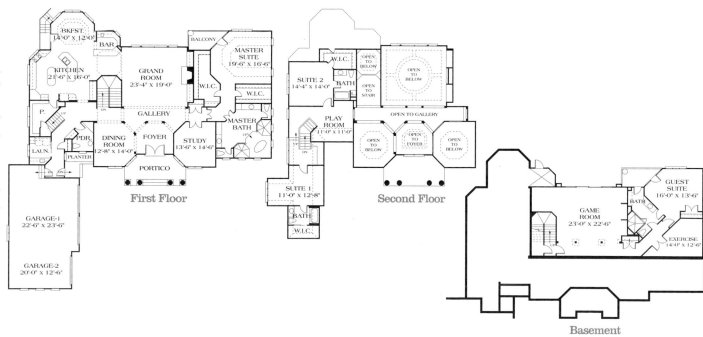

First Floor

Second Floor

Basement

Plan:
HPK1500274

Style:
MEDITERRANEAN

Square Footage:
3,508

Bedrooms:
3

Bathrooms:
4

Width:
75' - 0"

Depth:
104' - 10"

Foundation:
SLAB

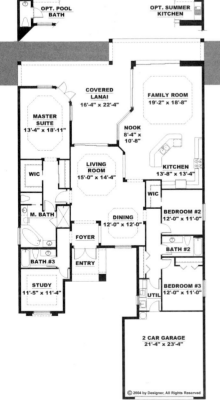

Plan:
HPK1500275

Style:
MEDITERRANEAN

Square Footage:
2,565

Width:
51' - 0"

Bedrooms:
3

Bathrooms:
3

Depth:
97' - 6"

Foundation:
SLAB

Plan:
HPK1500276

Style:
MEDITERRANEAN

First Floor:
4,536 SQ. FT.

Second Floor:
2,468 SQ. FT.

Total:
7,004 SQ. FT.

Bonus Space:
2,834 SQ. FT.

Bedrooms:
5

Bathrooms:
7 1/2

Width:
132' - 7"

Depth:
99' - 8"

Foundation:
FINISHED WALKOUT BASEMENT

From the porte cochere through the portico and into the foyer with a gorgeous semi-circular staircase, this European design oozes elegance. Multipaned windows and an attractive cupola over the garage further enhance the facade. A lively kitchen is situated near the family room past a bar, the hearth-warmed great room, and the dining room. The first-floor master suite is a study in opulance. Four more bedrooms—one with a sitting area—with private baths comprise the second floor. The lower level is devoted to relaxation and entertainment—check out the theater, exercise room, rec room, and massage room!

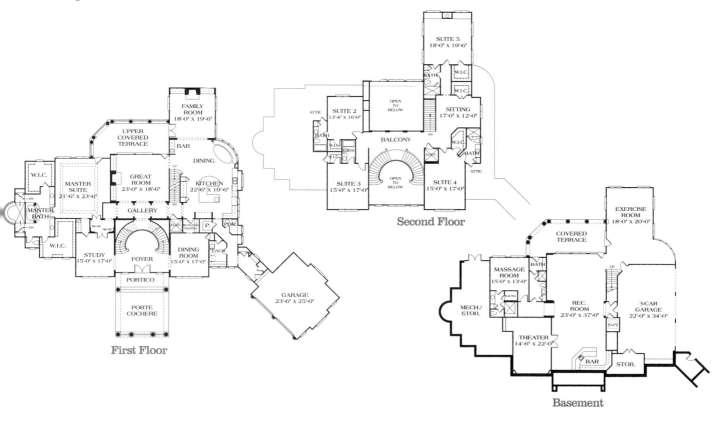

First Floor

Second Floor

Basement

Plan:
HPK1500277

Style:
MEDITERRANEAN

Square Footage:
2,259

Bedrooms:
4

Bathrooms:
3

Width:
59' - 8"

Depth:
54' - 4"

Foundation:
SLAB

Plan:
HPK1500278

Style:
MEDITERRANEAN

Square Footage:
2,259

Bedrooms:
4

Bathrooms:
3

Width:
59' - 8"

Depth:
54' - 4"

Foundation:
SLAB

Mediterranean & Spanish Styles

Plan:
HPK1500279

Style:
ITALIANATE

First Floor:
3,631 SQ. FT.

Second Floor:
2,195 SQ. FT.

Total:
5,826 SQ. FT.

Bonus Space:
822 SQ. FT.

Bedrooms:
5

Bathrooms:
4 1/2

Width:
101' - 4"

Depth:
92' - 6"

Foundation:
SLAB

This stucco Italianate masterpiece includes room for everything—then room to grow!
Four bedrooms and baths upstairs have their fun level boosted by two separate bonus
rooms, a loft, and a game room. The first-floor master suite, secluded on this level for
privacy, includes access to the covered rear porch. The den, dining room, and living
room provide a triumvirate of entertaining and relaxing options. A corner hearth and
space for all are found in the family room, sure to be a gathering place for family and
friends. The C-shaped, island kitchen with walk-in pantry combines convenient cooking space with plenty of storage.

First Floor

Second Floor

Mediterranean & Spanish Styles

Plan:
HPK1500280

Style:
EUROPEAN COTTAGE

First Floor:
2,163 SQ. FT.

Second Floor:
1,415 SQ. FT.

Total:
3,578 SQ. FT.

Bedrooms:
5

Bathrooms:
3 1/2

Width:
71' - 0"

Depth:
72' - 0"

Foundation:
SLAB

© The Sater Design Collection, Inc.

The arched portico, balcony, and low-pitched roof combine to form a pleasingly Italianate facade in this European design. Matching arches top front-facing windows. In the interior, the foyer opens into the great room, featuring a fireplace, built-in entertainment center, and access to the rear terrace. The left wing of the plan comprises the large island kitchen, dining room with beamed ceiling, and an airy breakfast nook. The right wing is reserved for the study, master suite, and master bath. Upstairs, four bedrooms share two full baths and access to the balcony. Art niches adorn the walls throughout the house.

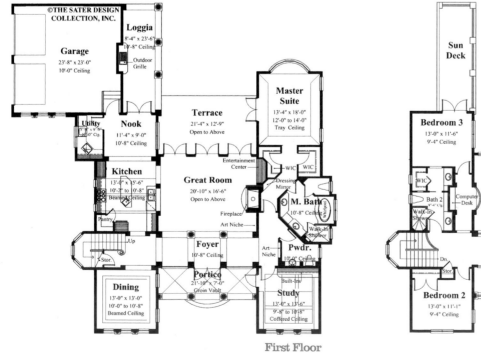

First Floor

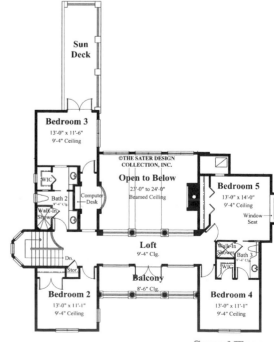

Second Floor

Mediterranean & Spanish Styles

First Floor

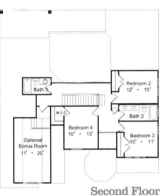

Second Floor

Plan:
HPK1500281

Style:
TRADITIONAL

First Floor:
1,796 SQ. FT.

Second Floor:
1,057 SQ. FT.

Total:
2,853 SQ. FT.

Bonus Space:
220 SQ. FT.

Bedrooms:
4

Bathrooms:
3 ½

Width:
50' - 0"

Depth:
56' - 0"

Foundation:
SLAB

Plan:
HPK1500282

Style: **ITALIANATE**	Total: **3,192 SQ. FT.**	Width: **53' - 0"**
First Floor: **2,335 SQ. FT.**	Bedrooms: **4**	Depth: **75' - 0"**
Second Floor: **857 SQ. FT.**	Bathrooms: **3 ½**	Foundation: **SLAB**

First Floor

Second Floor

Plan:
HPK1500283

Style:
MEDITERRANEAN

Square Footage:
3,490

Bedrooms:
4

Bathrooms:
4

Width:
69' - 8"

Depth:
115' - 0"

Foundation:
SLAB

*Photography courtesy of Scott Mitchum Photography.
This home, as shown in photographs, may differ from the actual blueprints.*

Plan:
HPK1500284

Style:	Bedrooms:	Depth:
INTERNATIONAL	**5**	**77' - 8"**
Square Footage:	Bathrooms:	Foundation:
5,106	**4 1/2**	**SLAB**
Bonus Space:	Width:	
508 SQ. FT.	**114' - 0"**	

Plan:
HPK1500285

Style:
CONTEMPORARY

First Floor:
3,214 SQ. FT.

Second Floor:
1,576 SQ. FT.

Total:
4,790 SQ. FT.

Bonus Space:
649 SQ. FT.

Bedrooms:
5

Bathrooms:
4 1/2

Width:
76' - 8"

Depth:
100' - 4"

Foundation:
SLAB

Mediterranean influence is readily apparent in the arches atop the covered front porch, three-car garage, and second-floor balcony. Two rear covered patios bring outdoor living close to home and are accessible from the family room, nook, living room, and master bedroom. The living room, dining room, and den form the triangular heart of the home. The kitchen is a cook's dream with miles of counter space, including an island for prep work or casual snacking. The master suite is on the first floor and includes a relaxing sitting area and a bathroom with a gorgeous tub under the front window. A first-floor bedroom with private bath and three family bedrooms upstairs ensure enough room for kids and guests to sleep comfortably. Finish the bonus room to take full advantage of that balcony!

First Floor

Second Floor

Plan:
HPK1500286

Style:
CONTEMPORARY

First Floor:
2,898 SQ. FT.

Second Floor:
441 SQ. FT.

Total:
3,339 SQ. FT.

Bedrooms:
4

Bathrooms:
4

Width:
80' - 0"

Depth:
67' - 0"

Foundation:
SLAB

Second Floor

First Floor

Plan:
HPK1500287

Style:
CONTEMPORARY

Square Footage:
2,089

Width:
61' - 8"

Bedrooms:
4

Bathrooms:
3

Depth:
50' - 4"

Foundation:
SLAB

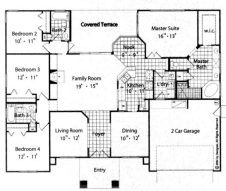

Plan:
HPK1500288

Style:
CONTEMPORARY

Square Footage:
2,362

Bedrooms:
3

Bathrooms:
3

Width:
65' - 8"

Depth:
73' - 4"

Foundation:
SLAB

Plan:
HPK1500289

Style:	Bedrooms:	Depth:
CONTEMPORARY	**3**	**59' - 0"**
Square Footage:	Bathrooms:	Foundation:
1,590	**2**	**SLAB**
	Width:	
	43' - 0"	

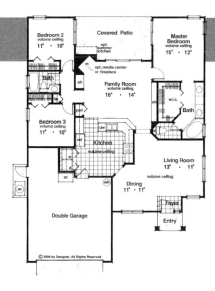

Alternate Exterior

Plan:
HPK1500290

Style:
CONTEMPORARY

Square Footage:
3,556

Bedrooms:
4

Bathrooms:
3 1/2

Width:
85' - 0"

Depth:
85' - 0"

Foundation:
SLAB

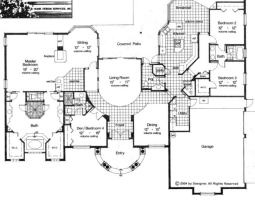

Plan:
HPK1500291

Style:
FLORIDIAN

Square Footage:
2,710

Width:
98' - 6"

Bedrooms:
3

Bathrooms:
3

Depth:
50' - 0"

Foundation:
SLAB

Plan:
HPK1500292

Style:
FRENCH

First Floor:
5,204 SQ. FT.

Second Floor:
1,055 SQ. FT.

Total:
6,259 SQ. FT.

Bedrooms:
3

Bathrooms:
5 1/2

Width:
95' - 0"

Depth:
103' - 10"

Foundation:
SLAB

With just over 6,000 square feet, mostly devoted to a single level, this plan is sprawling with cozy sections throughout. Under the arched entryway, enter to find a coffered ceiling in the foyer, dining room, and library. Straight ahead is the living room with a bumped-out window providing views of the spa-enhanced covered patio to the rear. The spacious island kitchen is to the left and is open to the family room and nook for ideal casual serving purposes. The master suite takes up the entire right wing and includes a lavish bath and exercise room. To the left of the plan are two bedrooms with full private baths. A kid's room and full bath and bonus space are on the second level. Two two-car garages ensure safety for the family fleet.

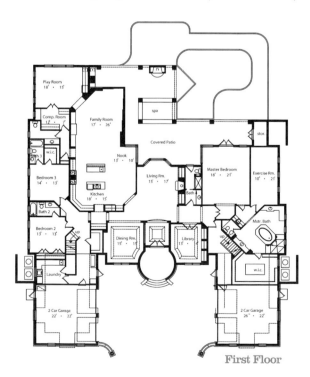

First Floor

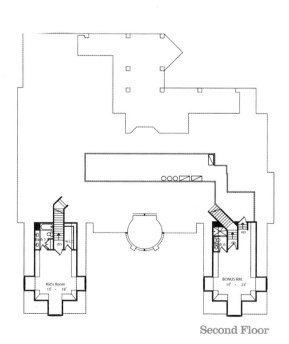

Second Floor

Plan:
HPK1500293

Style:
CONTEMPORARY

Square Footage:
2,376

Bedrooms:
4

Bathrooms:
3

Width:
59' - 6"

Depth:
72' - 0"

Foundation:
SLAB

Open, breezy, interior spaces are built for entertaining in this modern floor plan. The tile extends from the foyer through to the kitchen, utility room, breakfast area, and is found in each bathroom. The living room features a wet bar for special guests and double French doors to the large, rear patio. The master suite enjoys a sitting area, French doors to the patio, two walk-in closets, and a super bath. Three family bedrooms sit to the right of the floor plan and share two full baths. The family room is just off the kitchen and is a perfect spot to enjoy a fire and family gatherings.

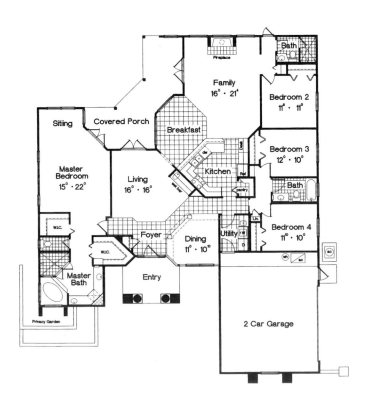

Mediterranean & Spanish Styles

Plan:
HPK1500295

Style:
ITALIANATE

First Floor:
3,465 SQ. FT.

Second Floor:
2,118 SQ. FT.

Total:
5,583 SQ. FT.

Bonus Space:
454 SQ. FT.

Bedrooms:
5

Bathrooms:
6 1/2

Width:
101' - 4"

Depth:
86' - 0"

Foundation:
SLAB

Arch-topped windows and doorways, a tiled roof, and window terraces are inspiring features of this Spanish-style home. Sunlight bathes the interior through plentiful windows and French doors in every room. Two complete levels of living; the first floor for casual and formal entertaining and the second floor for private living and recreation. The first-floor master suite is a work of spectacular comfort and seclusion. A gorgeous master bath includes compartmented commode and bidet, garden tub, shower enclosure, dual-sink vanity, a private courtyard view, and two walk-in closets. Above the twin two-car garages, future guest or staff quarters are available.

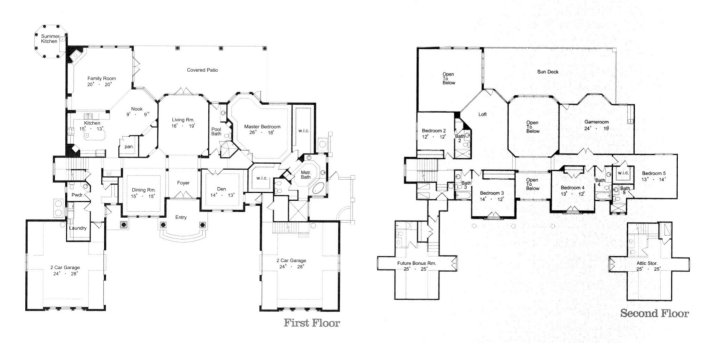

First Floor

Second Floor

Plan:
HPK1500294

Style:
CONTEMPORARY

Square Footage:
2,409

Bedrooms:
3

Bathrooms:
3

Width:
65' - 0"

Depth:
85' - 0"

Foundation:
SLAB

An elegant double-door entry opens to a a roomy gallery with the dining room to the right and the living room straight ahead. The large kitchen is accompanied by the breakfast room that opens to the spacious family room—with built-in and a fireplace. Two secondary bedrooms share a full bath. On the opposite side of the home, a private study is near the master suite. The master bedroom features a large sitting area and decorative ceiling. In the master bath, twin walk-in closets, dual-sink vanity, separate shower, and garden tub soothe the homeowners.

Mediterranean & Spanish Styles

325
New Home Plans

Plan:
HPK1500298

Style:
MEDITERRANEAN

First Floor:
4,825 SQ. FT.

Second Floor:
638 SQ. FT.

Total:
5,463 SQ. FT.

Bedrooms:
4

Bathrooms:
4 1/2

Width:
77' - 8"

Depth:
119' - 4"

Foundation:
SLAB

Spanish and Italian styles mingle their best details in this design. An arched entry is greeted by an interior colonnade defining the foyer, dining, and living rooms. Twin sets of French doors connect the porch to the inside extending living and entertaining space significantly. A great gourmet kitchen is outfitted with double islands and is open to the spacious family room and breakfast nook. A coffered ceiling and double doors dress up the den. Just off the den is the master suite, which features two walk-in closets each connected to dressing rooms complete with commode and vanity. The second floor has space for games and privacy. Two family bedrooms enjoy private baths, walk-in closets, game room, loft, a kitchenette, and large outside balcony.

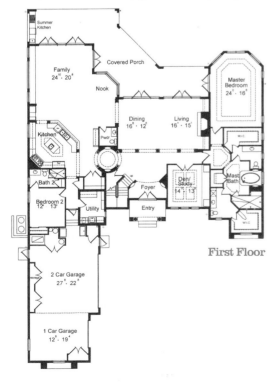

First Floor

Second Floor

Plan:
HPK1500296

Style:
MEDITERRANEAN

First Floor:
3,103 SQ. FT.

Second Floor:
1,616 SQ. FT.

Total:
4,719 SQ. FT.

Bedrooms:
4

Bathrooms:
3 1/2 + 1/2

Width:
86' - 9"

Depth:
84' - 6"

This two-story Southwestern design boasts an exciting layout and great ceilings. The family room soars at the heart of the plan, surrounded by an excellent kitchen and breakfast nook on one side and a turreted stairwell on the other. Octagonal dimensions in these larger rooms create interesting transitional spaces and niches between them and the bedrooms. The master suite commands the left of the plan and features a flow-through design terminating at a very large walk-in closet. The remaining three bedrooms reside upstairs.

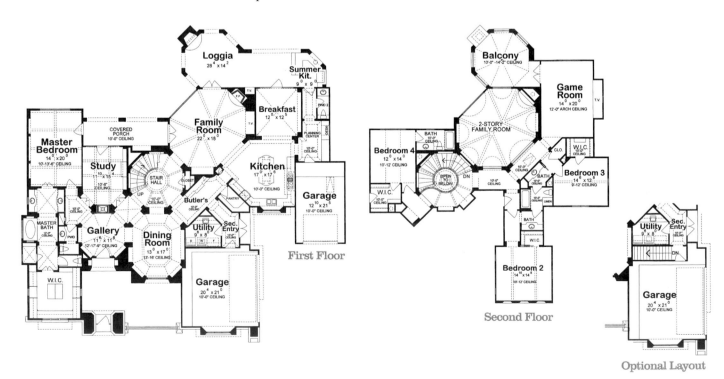

First Floor

Second Floor

Optional Layout

Plan:
HPK1500299

Style:
FRENCH COUNTRY

Square Footage:
3,064

Bonus Space:
366 SQ. FT.

Bedrooms:
4

Bathrooms:
4

Width:
79' - 6"

Depth:
91' - 0"

Foundation:
SLAB

This opulent French Chateau estate unfolds a dramatic interior with two layout choices. A formal entry is flanked by the beautiful dining room and a private den with coffered ceiling, built-ins, and double doors. The living room is an ideal space for after-dinner entertaining. A wet bar and corner fireplace warm up the space and the view of the pool adds light and color. Family spaces are not overlooked and the kitchen, eating nook, family room, and lanai are great recreation areas. The lanai provides an outdoor kitchen, convenient for snacks after a swim. Two secondary bedrooms share a Jack-and-Jill bath. An entire wing is dedicated to the master suite. Secluded luxury, the master bath includes an oversized walk-in closet, shower enclosure, soaking tub, dual-sink vanity, and a private garden courtyard.

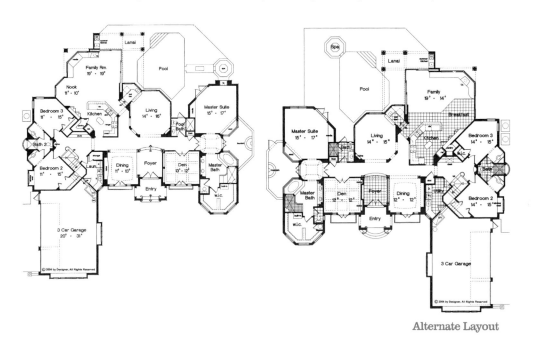

Alternate Layout

Plan:
HPK1500297

Style:
MEDITERRANEAN

First Floor:
3,148 SQ. FT.

Second Floor:
2,055 SQ. FT.

Total:
5,203 SQ. FT.

Bedrooms:
4

Bathrooms:
4 ¹/₂

Width:
75' - 4"

Depth:
73' - 9"

Foundation:
SLAB

Sun-washed Mediterranean style offers up a luxurious and intriguing interior and exterior details. An entry porch opens to a long arcade that borders a private courtyard. The spacious gallery greets visitors with a high-style circular staircase and unobstructed views of the formal dining room and attractive study. To the right, relax in solitude and grandeur as the master suite pampers you with ornate ceilings, a sitting bay, His and Hers dressing areas, separate shower and tub, and a room-sized walk-in closet. Splendid open spaces enhance interaction between the family room and large kitchen, which feature an adjoining eating area and planning center. A convenient wine room is a gourmet delight. Generous secondary bedrooms each feature a large walk-in closet, private bath, and access to a flexible game room and tower.

First Floor

Second Floor

Plan:
HPK1500300

Style:
MEDITERRANEAN

Main Level:
2,895 SQ. FT.

Upper Level:
905 SQ. FT.

Lower Level:
2,563 SQ. FT.

Total:
6,363 SQ. FT.

Bedrooms:
5

Bathrooms:
6 1/2

Width:
73' - 4"

Depth:
89' - 0"

Foundation:
FINISHED BASEMENT

To the left of the facade, paired windows on a white wall effect a subtle but certain Mediterranean style to this grand design. The same appreciation for naturalistic forms can be seen in the rounded hallway from the main dining room to the nook and kitchen. A luxurious master suite occupies the left side of the plan, with private access to the covered patio. Guests will enjoy similar comforts in interestingly shaped rooms and full baths.

This home, as shown in photographs, may differ from the actual blueprints. For more detailed information, please check the floor plans carefully.

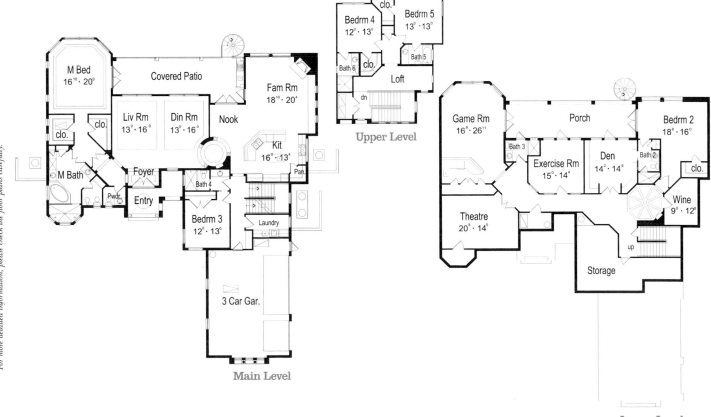

Turn Your
Dream Home
Into A *Reality*

ARTS & CRAFTS HOME PLANS
1-931131-26-0

$14.95 (128 PAGES)
This title showcases 85 home plans in the Craftsman, Prairie and Bungalow styles.

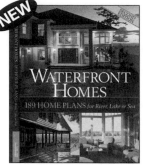

WATERFRONT HOMES
1-931131-28-7

$10.95 (208 PAGES)
A collection of gorgeous homes for those who dream of life on the water's edge—this title features open floor plans with expansive views.

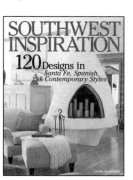

SOUTHWEST INSPIRATION
1-931131-19-8

$14.95 (192 PAGES)
This title features 120 designs in Santa Fe, Spanish and Contemporary styles.

SUN COUNTRY STYLES
1-931131-14-7

$9.95 (192 PAGES)
175 designs from Coastal Cottages to stunning Southwesterns.

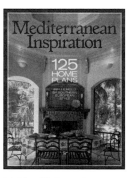

MEDITERRANEAN INSPIRATION
1-931131-09-0

$14.95 (192 PAGES)
Bring home the timeless beauty of the Mediterranean with the gorgeous plans featured in this popular title.

FARMHOUSE & COUNTRY PLANS
1-881955-77-X

$10.95 (320 PAGES)
Farmhouse & Country Plans features 300 fresh designs from classic to modern.

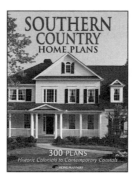

SOUTHERN COUNTRY HOME PLANS
1-931131-06-6

$10.95 (320 PAGES)
Southern Country Home Plans showcases 300 plans from Historic Colonials to Contemporary Coastals.

PROVENCAL INSPIRATION
1-881955-89-3

$14.95 (192 PAGES)
This title features home plans, landscapes and interior plans that evoke the French Country spirit.

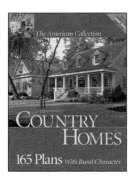

THE AMERICAN COLLECTION: COUNTRY HOMES
1-931131-35-X

$10.95 (192 PAGES)
The American Collection: Country is a must-have if you're looking to build a country home or if you want to bring the relaxed country spirit into your current home.

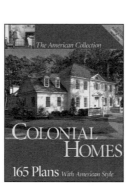

THE AMERICAN COLLECTION: COLONIAL HOMES
1-931131-40-6

$10.95 (192 PAGES)
This beautiful collection features distinctly American home styles— find everything from Colonials, Cape Cod, Georgian, Farmhouse to Saltbox.

PICK UP A COPY TODAY!

Toll-Free:
800.322.6797

Online:
http://books.eplans.com

Hanley Wood HomePlanners provides the largest selection of plans from the nation's top designers and architects. Our special home styles collection offers designs to suit any style.

HANLEY WOOD CONSUMER
One Thomas Circle, NW, Suite 600, Washington, DC 20005   NHP6

With more than 50 years of experience in the industry and millions of blueprints sold, Hanley Wood is a trusted source of high-quality, high-value pre-drawn home plans.

Using pre-drawn home plans is a **reliable, cost-effective way** to build your dream home, and our vast selection of plans is second-to-none. The nation's finest designers craft these plans that builders know they can trust. Meanwhile, our friendly, knowledgeable customer service representatives can help you every step of the way.

WHAT YOU'LL GET WITH YOUR ORDER

The contents of each designer's blueprint package is unique, but all contain detailed, high-quality working drawings. You can expect to find the following standard elements in most sets of plans:

I. FRONT PERSPECTIVE

This artist's sketch of the exterior of the house gives you an idea of how the house will look when built and landscaped.

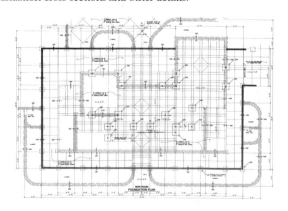

2. FOUNDATION AND BASEMENT PLANS

This sheet shows the foundation layout including concrete walls, footings, pads, posts, beams, bearing walls, and foundation notes. If the home features a basement, the first-floor framing details may also be included on this plan. If your plan features slab construction rather than a basement, the plan shows footings and details for a monolithic slab. This page, or another in the set, may include a sample plot plan for locating your house on a building site. Additional sheets focus on foundation cross-sections and other details.

3. DETAILED FLOOR PLANS

These plans show the layout of each floor of the house. Rooms and interior spaces are carefully dimensioned, doors and windows located, and keys are given for cross-section details provided elsewhere in the plans.

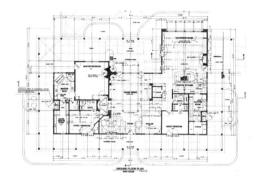

4. HOUSE AND DETAIL CROSS-SECTIONS

Large-scale views show sections or cutaways of the foundation, interior walls, exterior walls, floors, stairways, and roof details. Additional cross-sections may show important changes in floor, ceiling, or roof heights, or the relationship of one level to another. These sections show exactly how the various parts of the house fit together and are extremely valuable during construction. Additional sheets may include enlarged wall, floor, and roof construction details.

5. ROOF AND FLOOR STRUCTURAL SUPPORTS

The roof and floor framing plans provide detail for these crucial elements of your home. Each includes floor joist, ceiling joist, rafter and roof joist size, spacing, direction, span, and specifications. Beam and window headers, along with necessary details for framing connections, stairways, skylights, or dormers are also included.

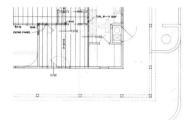

6. ELECTRICAL PLAN

The electrical plan offers a detailed outline of all wiring for your home, with notes for all lighting, outlets, switches, and circuits. A layout is provided for each level, as well as basements, garages, or other structures.

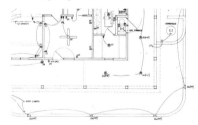

7. EXTERIOR ELEVATIONS

In addition to the front exterior, your blueprint set will include drawings of the rear and sides of your house as well. These drawings give notes on exterior materials and finishes. Particular attention is given to cornice detail, brick and stone accents, or other finish items that make your home unique.

BEFORE YOU CALL

You are making a terrific decision to use a pre-drawn house plan—it is one you can make with confidence, knowing that your blueprints are crafted by national-award-winning certified residential designers and architects, and trusted by builders.

Once you've selected the plan you want—or even if you have questions along the way—our experienced customer service representatives are available 24 hours a day, seven days a week to help you navigate the home-building process. To help them provide you with even better service, please consider the following questions before you call:

■ Have you chosen or purchased your lot?
If so, please review the building setback requirements of your local building authority before you call. You don't need to have a lot before ordering plans, but if you own land already, please have the width and depth dimensions handy when you call.

■ Have you chosen a builder?
Involving your builder in the plan selection and evaluation process may be beneficial. Luckily, builders know they can have confidence with pre-drawn plans because they've been designed for livability, functionality, and typically are builder-proven at successful home sites across the country.

■ Do you need a construction loan?
Construction loans are unique because they involve determining the value of something that is not yet constructed. Several lenders offer convenient contstruction-to-permanent loans. It is important to choose a good lending partner—one who will help guide you through the application and appraisal process. Most will even help you evaluate your contractor to ensure reliability and credit worthiness. Our partnership with IndyMac Bank, a nationwide leader in construction loans, can help you save on your loan, if needed.

■ How many sets of plans do you need?
Building a home can typically require a number of sets of blueprints—one for yourself, two or three for the builder and subcontractors, two for the local building department, and one or more for your lender. For this reason, we offer 5- and 8-set plan packages, but your best value is the Reproducible Plan Package. Reproducible plans are accompanied by a license to make modifications and typically up to 12 duplicates of the plan so you have enough copies of the plan for everyone involved in the financing and construction of your home.

■ Do you want to make any changes to the plan?
We understand that it is difficult to find blueprints for a home that will meet all of your needs. That is why Hanley Wood is glad to offer plan Customization Services. We will work with you to design the modifications you'd like to see and to adjust your blueprint plans accordingly—anything from changing the foundation; adding square footage, redesigning baths, kitchens, or bedrooms; or most other modifications. This simple, cost-effective service saves you from hiring an outside architect to make alterations. Modifications may only be made to Reproducible Plan Packages that include the license to modify.

■ Do you have to make any changes to meet local building codes?
While all of our plans are drawn to meet national building codes at the time they were created, many areas required that plans be stamped by a local engineer to certify that they meet local building codes. Building codes are updated frequently and can vary by state, county, city, or municipality. Contact your local building inspection department, office of planning and zoning, or department of permits to determine how your local codes will affect your construction project. The best way to assure that you can make changes to your plan, if necessary, is to purchase a Reproducible Plan Package.

■ Has everyone—from family members to contractors—been involved in selecting the plan?
Building a new home is an exciting process, and using pre-drawn plans is a great way to realize your dreams. Make sure that everyone involved has had an opportunity to review the plan you've selected. While Hanley Wood is the only plans provider with an exchange policy, it's best to be sure all parties agree on your selection before you buy.

CALL TOLL-FREE 1-800-521-6797

Source Key
HPK15

CUSTOMIZE YOUR PLAN – HANLEY WOOD CUSTOMIZATION SERVICES

Creating custom home plans has never been easier and more directly accessible. Using state-of-the-art technology and top-performing architectural expertise, Hanley Wood delivers on a long-standing customer commitment to provide world-class home-plans and customization services. Our valued customers—professional home builders and individual home owners—appreciate the convenience and accessibility of this interactive, consultative service.

With the Hanley Wood Customization Service you can:
■ Save valuable time by avoiding drawn-out and frequently repetitive face-to-face design meetings
■ Communicate design and home-plan changes faster and more efficiently
■ Speed-up project turn-around time
■ Build on a budget without sacrificing quality
■ Transform master home plans to suit your design needs and unique personal style

All of our design options and prices are impressively affordable. A detailed quote is available for a $50 consultation fee. Plan modification is an interactive service. Our skilled team of designers will guide you through the customization process from start to finish making recommendations, offering ideas, and determining the feasibility of your changes. This level of service is offered to ensure the final modified plan meets your expectations. If you use our service the $50 fee will be applied to the cost of the modifications.

You may purchase the customization consultation before or after purchasing a plan. In either case, it is necessary to purchase the Reproducible Plan Package and complete the accompanying license to modify the plan before we can begin customization.

Customization Consultation $50

TOOLS TO WORK WITH YOUR BUILDER

Two Reverse Options For Your Convenience – Mirror and Right-Reading Reverse (as available)
Mirror reverse plans simply flip the design 180 degrees—keep in mind, the text will also be flipped. For a minimal fee you can have one or all of your plans shipped mirror reverse, although we recommend having at least one regular set handy. Right-reading reverse plans show the design flipped 180 degrees but the text reads normally. When you choose this option, we ship each set of purchased blueprints in this format.

Mirror Reverse Fee (indicate the number of sets when ordering). . . . **$55**
Right Reading Reverse Fee (all sets are reversed). **$175**

A Shopping List Exclusively for Your Home – Materials List
A customized Materials List helps you plan and estimate the cost of your new home, outlining the quantity, type, and size of materials needed to build your house (with the exception of mechanical system items). Included are framing lumber, windows and doors, kitchen and bath cabinetry, rough and finished hardware, and much more.

Materials List . . . .**$75 each**
Additional Materials Lists (at original time of purchase only). . **$20 each**

Plan Your Home-Building Process – Specification Outline
Work with your builder on this step-by-step chronicle of 166 stages or items crucial to the building process. It provides a comprehensive review of the construction process and helps you choose materials.
Specification Outline . . . .**$10 each**

Get Accurate Cost Estimates for Your Home – Quote One® Cost Reports
The Summary Cost Report, the first element in the Quote One® package, breaks down the cost of your home into various categories based on building materials, labor, and installation, and includes three grades of construction: Budget, Standard, and Custom. Make even more informed decisions about your project with the second element of our package, the Material Cost Report. The material and installation cost is shown for each of more than 1,000 line items provided in the standard-grade Materials List, which is included with this tool. Additional space is included for estimates from contractors and subcontractors, such as for mechanical materials, which are not included in our packages.

Quote One® Summary Cost Report **$35**
Quote One® Detailed Material Cost Report **$140***
***Detailed material cost report includes the Materials List**

Learn the Basics of Building – Electrical, Plumbing, Mechanical, Construction Detail Sheets
If you want to know more about building techniques—and deal more confidently with your subcontractors—we offer four useful detail sheets. These sheets provide non-plan-specific general information, but are excellent tools that will add to your understanding of Plumbing Details, Electrical Details, Construction Details, and Mechanical Details.

Electrical Detail Sheet **$14.95**
Plumbing Detail Sheet **$14.95**
Mechanical Detail Sheet **$14.95**
Construction Detail Sheet **$14.95**
SUPER VALUE SETS:
Buy any 2: $26.95; Buy any 3: $34.95; Buy All 4: $39.95

Best Value

MAKE YOUR HOME TECH-READY — HOME AUTOMATION UPGRADE

Building a new home provides a unique opportunity to wire it with a plan for future needs. A Home Automation-Ready (HA-Ready) home contains the wiring substructure of tomorrow's connected home. It means that every room—from the front porch to the backyard, and from the attic to the basement—is wired for security, lighting, telecommunications, climate control, home computer networking, whole-house audio, home theater, shade control, video surveillance, entry access control, and yes, video gaming electronic solutions.

Along with the conveniences HA-Ready homes provide, they also have a higher resale value. The Consumer Electronics Association (CEA), in conjunction with the Custom Electronic Design and Installation Association (CEDIA), have developed a TechHome™ Rating system that quantifies the value of HA-Ready homes. The rating system is gaining widespread recognition in the real estate industry.

Developed by CEDIA-certified installers, our Home Automation Upgrade package includes everything you need to work with an installer during the construction of your home. It provides a short explanation of the various subsystems, a wiring floor plan for each level of your home, a detailed materials list with estimated costs, and a list of CEDIA-certified installers in your local area.

Home Automation Upgrade $250

GET YOUR HOME PLANS PAID FOR!

IndyMac Bank, in partnership with Hanley Wood, will reimburse you up to $600 toward the cost of your home plans simply by financing the construction of your new home with IndyMac Bank Home Construction Lending.

IndyMac's construction and permanent loan is a one-time close loan, meaning that one application—and one set of closing fees—provides all the financing you need.

Apply today at www.indymacbank.com, call toll free at 1-866-237-3478, or ask a Hanley Wood customer service representative for details.

DESIGN YOUR HOME — INTERIOR AND EXTERIOR FINISHING TOUCHES

Be Your Own Interior Designer! — Home Furniture Planner

Effectively plan the space in your home using our Hands-On Home Furniture Planner. It's fun and easy—no more moving heavy pieces of furniture to see how the room will go together. The kit includes reusable peel-and-stick furniture templates that fit on a 12"x18" laminated layout board—enough space to lay out every room in your house.

Home Furniture Planning Kit **$15.95**

Enjoy the Outdoors! — Deck Plans

Many of our homes have a corresponding deck plan, sold separately, which includes a Deck Plan Frontal Sheet, Deck Framing and Floor Plans, Deck Elevations, and a Deck Materials List. A Standard Deck Details Package, also available, provides all the how-to information necessary for building any deck. Get both the Deck Plan and the Standard Deck Details Package for one low price in our Complete Deck Building Package. See the price tier chart below and call for deck plan availability.

Deck Details (only) **$14.95**
Deck Building Package . . . . **Plan price + $14.95**

Create a Professionally Designed Landscape — Landscape Plans

Many of our homes have a front-yard Landscape Plan that is complementary in design to the house plan. These comprehensive Landscape Blueprint Packages include a Frontal Sheet, Plan View, Regionalized Plant & Materials List, a sheet on Planting and Maintaining Your Landscape, Zone Maps, and a Plant Size and Description Guide. Each set of blueprints is a full 18" x 24" with clear, complete instructions in easy-to-read type. Our Landscape Plans are available with a Plant & Materials List adapted by horticultural experts to eight regions of the country. Please specify your region when ordering your plan—see region map below. Call for more information about landscape plan availability and applicable regions.

LANDSCAPE & DECK PRICE SCHEDULE

PRICE TIERS	1-SET STUDY PACKAGE	5-SET BUILDING PACKAGE	8-SET BUILDING PACKAGE	1-SET REPRODUCIBLE*
P1	$25	$55	$95	$145
P2	$45	$75	$115	$165
P3	$75	$105	$145	$195
P4	$105	$135	$175	$225
P5	$145	$175	$215	$275
P6	$185	$215	$255	$315

PRICES SUBJECT TO CHANGE   * REQUIRES A FAX NUMBER

TERMS & CONDITIONS

OUR 90-DAY EXCHANGE POLICY

Hanley Wood is committed to ensuring your satisfaction with your blueprint order, which is why we offer a 90-day exchange policy. With the exception of Reproducible Plan Package orders, we will exchange your entire first order for an equal or greater number of blueprints from our plan collection within 90 days of the original order. The entire content of your original order must be returned before an exchange will be processed. Please call our customer service department at 1-888-690-1116 for your return authorization number and shipping instructions. If the returned blueprints look used, redlined, or copied, we will not honor your exchange. Fees for exchanging your blueprints are as follows: 20% of the amount of the original order, plus the difference in cost if exchanging for a design in a higher price bracket or less the difference in cost if exchanging for a design in a lower price bracket. (Because they can be copied, Reproducible blueprints are not exchangeable or refundable.) Please call for current postage and handling prices. Shipping and handling charges are not refundable.

ARCHITECTURAL AND ENGINEERING SEALS

Some cities and states now require that a licensed architect or engineer review and "seal" a blueprint, or officially approve it, prior to construction. Prior to application for a building permit or the start of actual construction, we strongly advise that you consult your local building official who can tell you if such a review is required.

LOCAL BUILDING CODES AND ZONING REQUIREMENTS

Each plan was designed to meet or exceed the requirements of a nationally recognized model building code in effect at the time and place the plan was drawn. Typically plans designed after the year 2000 conform to the International Residential Building Code (IRC 2000 or 2003). The IRC is comprised of portions of the three major codes below. Plans drawn before 2000 conform to one of the three recognized building codes in effect at the time: Building Officials and Code Administrators (BOCA) International, Inc.;

CALL TOLL-FREE 1-800-521-6797 OR VISIT EPLANS.COM

the Southern Building Code Congress International, (SBCCI) Inc.; the International Conference of Building Officials (ICBO); or the Council of American Building Officials (CABO).

Because of the great differences in geography and climate throughout the United States and Canada, each state, county, and municipality has its own building codes, zone requirements, ordinances, and building regulations. Your plan may need to be modified to comply with local requirements. In addition, you may need to obtain permits or inspections from local governments before and in the course of construction. We authorize the use of the blueprints on the express condition that you consult a local licensed architect or engineer of your choice prior to beginning construction and strictly comply with all local building codes, zoning requirements, and other applicable laws, regulations, ordinances, and requirements. Notice: Plans for homes to be built in Nevada must be redrawn by a Nevada-registered professional. Consult your local building official for more information on this subject.

TERMS AND CONDITIONS

These designs are protected under the terms of United States Copyright Law and may not be copied or reproduced in any way, by

any means, unless you have purchased a Reproducible Plan Package and signed the accompanying license to modify and copy the plan, which clearly indicates your right to modify, copy, or reproduce. We authorize the use of your chosen design as an aid in the construction of ONE (1) single- or multifamily home only. You may not use this design to build a second dwelling or multiple dwellings without purchasing another blueprint or blueprints or paying additional design fees. Multi-use fees vary by designer—please call one of experienced sales representatives for a quote.

DISCLAIMER

The designers we work with have put substantial care and effort into the creation of their blueprints. However, because we cannot provide on-site consultation, supervision, and control over actual construction, and because of the great variance in local building requirements, building practices, and soil, seismic, weather, and other conditions, WE MAKE NO WARRANTY OF ANY KIND, EXPRESS OR IMPLIED, WITH RESPECT TO THE CONTENT OR USE OF THE BLUEPRINTS, INCLUDING BUT NOT LIMITED TO ANY WARRANTY OF MERCHANTABILITY OR OF FITNESS FOR A PARTICULAR PURPOSE. ITEMS, PRICES, TERMS, AND CONDITIONS ARE SUBJECT TO CHANGE WITHOUT NOTICE.

IMPORTANT COPYRIGHT NOTICE

From the Council of Publishing Home Designers

Blueprints for residential construction (or working drawings, as they are often called in the industry) are copyrighted intellectual property, protected under the terms of the United States Copyright Law and, therefore, cannot be copied legally for use in building. The following are some guidelines to help you get what you need to build your home, without violating copyright law:

1. HOME PLANS ARE COPY-RIGHTED

Just like books, movies, and songs, home plans receive protection under the federal copyright laws. The copyright laws prevent anyone, other than the copyright owner, from reproducing, modifying, or reusing the plans or design without permission of the copyright owner.

2. DO NOT COPY DESIGNS OR FLOOR PLANS FROM ANY PUBLICATION, ELECTRONIC MEDIA, OR EXISTING HOME

It is illegal to copy, change, or redraw home designs found in a plan book, CDROM or on the Internet. The right to modify plans is one of the exclusive rights of copyright. It is also illegal to copy or redraw a constructed home that is protected by copyright, even if you have never seen the plans for the home. If you find a plan or home that you like, you must purchase a set of plans from an authorized source. The plans may not be lent, given away, or sold by the purchaser.

3. DO NOT USE PLANS TO BUILD MORE THAN ONE HOUSE

The original purchaser of house plans is typically licensed to build a single home from the plans. Building more than one home from the plans without permission is an infringement of the home designer's copyright. The purchase of a multiple-set package of plans is for the construction of a single home only. The purchase of additional sets of plans does not grant the right to construct more than one home.

4. HOUSE PLANS IN THE FORM OF BLUEPRINTS OR BLACKLINES CANNOT BE COPIED OR REPRODUCED

Plans, blueprints, or blacklines, unless they are reproducibles, cannot be copied or reproduced without prior written consent of the copyright owner. Copy shops and blueprinters are prohibited from making copies of these plans without the copyright release letter you receive with reproducible plans.

5. HOUSE PLANS IN THE FORM OF BLUEPRINTS OR BLACKLINES CANNOT BE REDRAWN

Plans cannot be modified or redrawn without first obtaining the copyright owner's permission. With your purchase of plans, you are licensed to make non-structural changes by "red-lining" the purchased plans. If you need to make structural changes or need to redraw the plans for any reason, you must purchase a reproducible set of plans (see topic 6) which includes a license to modify the plans. Blueprints do not come with a license to make structural changes or to redraw the plans. You may not reuse or sell the modified design.

6. REPRODUCIBILE HOME PLANS

Reproducible plans (for example sepias, mylars, CAD files, electronic files, and vellums) come with a license to make modifications to the plans. Once modified, the plans can be taken to a local copy shop or blueprinter to make up to 10 or 12 copies of the plans to use in the construction of a single home. Only one home can be constructed from any single purchased set of reproducible plans either in original form or as modified. The license to modify and copy must be completed and returned before the plan will be shipped.

7. MODIFIED DESIGNS CANNOT BE REUSED

Even if you are licensed to make modifications to a copyrighted design, the modified design is not free from the original designer's copyright. The sale or reuse of the modified design is prohibited. Also, be aware that any modification to plans relieves the original designer from liability for design defects and voids all warranties expressed or implied.

8. WHO IS RESPONSIBLE FOR COPYRIGHT INFRINGEMENT?

Any party who participates in a copyright violation may be responsible including the purchaser, designers, architects, engineers, drafters, homeowners, builders, contractors, sub-contractors, copy shops, blueprinters, developers, and real estate agencies. It does not matter whether or not the individual knows that a violation is being committed. Ignorance of the law is not a valid defense.

9. PLEASE RESPECT HOME DESIGN COPYRIGHTS

In the event of any suspected violation of a copyright, or if there is any uncertainty about the plans purchased, the publisher, architect, designer, or the Council of Publishing Home Designers (www.cphd.org) should be contacted before proceeding. Awards are sometimes offered for information about home design copyright infringement.

10. PENALTIES FOR INFRINGEMENT

Penalties for violating a copyright may be severe. The responsible parties are required to pay actual damages caused by the infringement (which may be substantial), plus any profits made by the infringer commissions to include all profits from the sale of any home built from an infringing design. The copyright law also allows for the recovery of statutory damages, which may be as high as $150,000 for each infringement. Finally, the infringer may be required to pay legal fees which often exceed the damages.

PLAN #	PRICE TIER	PAGE	MATERIALS LIST	QUOTE ONE®	DECK	DECK PRICE	LANDSCAPE	LANDSCAPE PRICE	REGIONS
HPK1500001	C2	8	Y						
HPK1500007	C3	12							
HPK1500008	C2	13	Y						
HPK1500009	A3	14							
HPK1500010	C3	15	Y						
HPK1500305	A4	16							
HPK1500306	L1	17	Y						
HPK1500301	C4	18							
HPK1500012	C3	19							
HPK1500303	L2	20							
HPK1500004	A3	21							
HPK1500013	A4	22							
HPK1500014	C1	23							
HPK1500015	C2	24							
HPK1500016	A4	25							
HPK1500307	C2	26							
HPK1500017	C2	27	Y						
HPK1500018	C2	28							
HPK1500302	C4	29							
HPK1500019	C4	30							
HPK1500002	A3	31	Y						
HPK1500020	L4	32							
HPK1500021	L1	33							
HPK1500003	C1	34							
HPK1500005	A4	34							
HPK1500330	C1	35							
HPK1500024	C4	36							
HPK1500025	C3	37							
HPK1500026	A4	38	Y						
HPK1500027	C1	38	Y						
HPK1500028	C1	39	Y						
HPK1500029	A4	40							
HPK1500030	C4	41	Y						
HPK1500031	C4	42	Y						
HPK1500032	A4	42							
HPK1500033	C1	43							
HPK1500034	C1	43							
HPK1500035	A1	44	Y						
HPK1500036	A4	44	Y						
HPK1500308	C1	45	Y						
HPK1500037	A4	46							
HPK1500038	A2	46							
HPK1500039	A3	47							
HPK1500040	C1	48							
HPK1500041	A4	48							
HPK1500042	C1	49							
HPK1500043	C1	50	Y						
HPK1500044	A3	50	Y						
HPK1500045	A3	51							
HPK1500046	C2	51							
HPK1500047	L2	52							
HPK1500309	A3	53							
HPK1500310	A3	53	Y						
HPK1500048	C1	54							
HPK1500049	A3	54	Y						
HPK1500050	A3	55							
HPK1500051	A2	56							
HPK1500052	C1	56							
HPK1500053	A2	57							
HPK1500054	C1	58	Y						
HPK1500055	C1	58							
HPK1500056	C1	59							
HPK1500057	C1	59							
HPK1500058	C1	60							
HPK1500059	C1	60							
HPK1500060	C1	61							
HPK1500061	A4	61							
HPK1500062	A4	62							
HPK1500063	C1	63							
HPK1500064	C2	63	Y						
HPK1500311	A4	64							
HPK1500065	A2	65	Y						
HPK1500066	A3	65	Y						
HPK1500067	A3	66							
HPK1500068	C4	67							
HPK1500312	C1	68							
HPK1500313	A3	68	Y						
HPK1500069	L2	69							
HPK1500070	A4	70							
HPK1500071	L2	71							
HPK1500072	C1	72							
HPK1500314	A3	73							
HPK1500073	C1	74							
HPK1500074	C1	74							
HPK1500075	L1	75							
HPK1500076	C1	76							
HPK1500077	C1	76							
HPK1500078	C3	77							
HPK1500079	C1	78							
HPK1500080	C1	78							
HPK1500081	C2	79							
HPK1500082	C3	80							
HPK1500083	C3	80							
HPK1500084	A3	81							
HPK1500315	A3	82							
HPK1500085	C3	83							
HPK1500086	C3	84							
HPK1500087	C3	85							
HPK1500088	A2	86							
HPK1500089	A2	86							
HPK1500090	A3	87							
HPK1500091	A2	87							
HPK1500092	A3	88							
HPK1500093	C1	89	Y						
HPK1500094	A2	89	Y						
HPK1500095	A2	90							
HPK1500096	A2	91	Y						
HPK1500097	C2	92	Y						
HPK1500329	A4	93							
HPK1500098	A3	94							

PLAN #	PRICE TIER	PAGE	MATERIALS LIST	QUOTE ONE®	DECK	DECK PRICE	LANDSCAPE	LANDSCAPE PRICE	REGIONS
HPK1500099	C1	94							
HPK1500100	C1	95							
HPK1500316	C1	95							
HPK1500101	A3	96	Y						
HPK1500102	A3	96							
HPK1500103	A4	97							
HPK1500104	A4	98							
HPK1500105	A2	98							
HPK1500106	C1	99							
HPK1500107	A3	99	Y						
HPK1500108	A4	100							
HPK1500109	A3	100							
HPK1500110	C2	101	Y						
HPK1500111	C1	102							
HPK1500112	C3	102							
HPK1500113	C2	103	Y						
HPK1500114	A4	104	Y						
HPK1500115	C2	104	Y						
HPK1500116	A4	105							
HPK1500117	C2	106	Y						
HPK1500118	C1	106	Y						
HPK1500119	C3	107	Y						
HPK1500120	C1	107	Y						
HPK1500121	C1	108							
HPK1500122	A4	109							
HPK1500123	C1	109	Y						
HPK1500124	C1	110	Y						
HPK1500125	C1	111							
HPK1500126	C2	111							
HPK1500127	C3	112							
HPK1500128	L1	113							
HPK1500129	C3	114							
HPK1500130	C2	115							
HPK1500131	C2	116							
HPK1500132	A3	116	Y						
HPK1500133	C3	117							
HPK1500134	A3	118							
HPK1500135	A2	118							
HPK1500136	C3	119							
HPK1500137	A4	120							
HPK1500138	A4	120							
HPK1500139	C3	121							
HPK1500140	C3	122							
HPK1500141	C4	123							
HPK1500142	C2	124							
HPK1500143	C1	124							
HPK1500144	C3	125							
HPK1500145	C3	126							
HPK1500146	C3	127							
HPK1500147	A2	128	Y						
HPK1500148	A4	128	Y						
HPK1500149	C3	129							
HPK1500150	L1	130							
HPK1500151	C1	131							
HPK1500317	C1	132	Y						
HPK1500318	C1	132							
HPK1500152	A4	133	Y						
HPK1500153	A4	134							
HPK1500154	A4	134							
HPK1500155	A4	135							
HPK1500156	A3	136							
HPK1500157	A3	136							
HPK1500158	A4	137							
HPK1500159	C1	138							
HPK1500160	C3	138							
HPK1500161	C1	139							
HPK1500162	C2	140							
HPK1500163	C2	141							
HPK1500164	L2	142							
HPK1500165	C4	143							
HPK1500319	C1	144	Y						
HPK1500320	C1	144	Y						
HPK1500166	C2	145							
HPK1500321	C1	145	Y						
HPK1500167	C1	146							
HPK1500168	C1	146	Y						
HPK1500169	C2	147							
HPK1500322	A4	147	Y						
HPK1500170	C1	148							
HPK1500171	A3	148	Y						
HPK1500172	A3	149	Y						
HPK1500173	A4	149							
HPK1500174	A4	150							
HPK1500323	A4	150	Y						
HPK1500175	A3	151							
HPK1500176	A3	151							
HPK1500177	C2	152							
HPK1500178	C2	152							
HPK1500179	A4	153							
HPK1500180	C3	154							
HPK1500181	C3	154							
HPK1500182	A4	155							
HPK1500183	C2	155							
HPK1500184	C2	156							
HPK1500185	C2	157							
HPK1500324	C1	158	Y						
HPK1500186	C2	159							
HPK1500187	A4	160							
HPK1500188	C3	161							
HPK1500189	A3	161							
HPK1500190	C4	162							
HPK1500191	C3	163							
HPK1500192	C1	164							
HPK1500193	C4	165							
HPK1500194	C3	165							
HPK1500195	C3	166							
HPK1500196	A3	166	Y						
HPK1500325	A4	167	Y						
HPK1500197	A3	168	Y						
HPK1500198	A4	169							

PLAN #	PRICE TIER	PAGE	MATERIALS LIST	QUOTE ONE®	DECK	DECK PRICE	LANDSCAPE	LANDSCAPE PRICE	REGIONS
HPK1500199	C1	170							
HPK1500326	SQ1	171							
HPK1500200	C3	172							
HPK1500201	L2	172							
HPK1500202	C2	173							
HPK1500203	L2	174							
HPK1500204	L1	175							
HPK1500205	C4	176							
HPK1500206	A4	176	Y						
HPK1500207	C4	177							
HPK1500208	L1	178							
HPK1500209	A4	179							
HPK1500210	C1	179							
HPK1500211	A4	180							
HPK1500006	C1	181							
HPK1500212	C1	181							
HPK1500214	A4	182							
HPK1500215	C1	182							
HPK1500216	A3	183							
HPK1500217	A3	183							
HPK1500218	C1	184							
HPK1500219	C4	185							
HPK1500220	C1	186							
HPK1500327	C2	187							
HPK1500221	C4	188							
HPK1500222	SQ1	189							
HPK1500223	C1	190	Y						
HPK1500224	C4	190							
HPK1500225	L1	191							
HPK1500226	L1	192							
HPK1500227	C1	192							
HPK1500228	C1	193							
HPK1500229	C1	193							
HPK1500230	L3	194							
HPK1500231	C4	195							
HPK1500232	C1	195							
HPK1500233	L1	196							
HPK1500234	L1	197							
HPK1500235	A4	198							
HPK1500236	C4	198							
HPK1500237	C4	199							
HPK1500238	A3	200							
HPK1500239	A3	200							
HPK1500240	SQ5	201							
HPK1500241	C1	202							
HPK1500242	C3	202							
HPK1500243	L2	203							
HPK1500244	L1	204							
HPK1500245	L1	204							
HPK1500328	A4	205							
HPK1500304	A4	206							
HPK1500247	C2	207							
HPK1500248	C2	207	Y						
HPK1500249	C4	208							
HPK1500250	C2	208							
HPK1500251	C3	209							
HPK1500252	C4	210							
HPK1500253	C2	210							
HPK1500254	L1	211							
HPK1500255	L3	212							
HPK1500256	SQ1	213							
HPK1500257	C4	214							
HPK1500258	SQ5	214	Y						
HPK1500259	SQ5	215	Y						
HPK1500260	C2	216							
HPK1500261	C3	216							
HPK1500262	SQ5	217							
HPK1500263	SQ3	218							
HPK1500264	SQ1	219							
HPK1500265	C1	220							
HPK1500266	C3	220							
HPK1500267	L2	221							
HPK1500268	SQ1	222							
HPK1500269	C2	223							
HPK1500270	A4	223							
HPK1500271	A4	224							
HPK1500272	C3	224							
HPK1500273	L3	225							
HPK1500274	C3	226							
HPK1500275	C1	226							
HPK1500276	L3	227							
HPK1500277	C2	228							
HPK1500278	C2	228							
HPK1500279	L2	229							
HPK1500280	L1	230							
HPK1500281	C1	231							
HPK1500282	C2	231							
HPK1500283	SQ1	232							
HPK1500284	L1	232							
HPK1500285	L1	233							
HPK1500286	SQ1	234							
HPK1500287	A4	234							
HPK1500288	A4	235							
HPK1500289	A3	235							
HPK1500290	C4	236	Y						
HPK1500291	C1	236							
HPK1500292	L2	237							
HPK1500293	A4	238							
HPK1500295	L2	239							
HPK1500294	A4	240							
HPK1500298	L1	241							
HPK1500296	C4	242							
HPK1500299	C3	243	Y						
HPK1500297	L1	244							
HPK1500300	SQ1	245							